FINDING OUR HAPPINESS FLOW

BY
DR. ROBERT PUFF, PH.D.

Published by eBookIt.com

ISBN-13: 978-1-4566-2580-1

Table of Contents

Introduction

We live in a society focused on want. We want a great career, we want money, we want a wonderful soulmate, we want to succeed . . .

You have probably picked up this book because you want to be happy. That is the basis of what everyone *truly* wants. The good news is that you don't need anyone or anything outside yourself to make it happen. You already have what you need, and it is inside you.

My hope is that all my writings about the pursuit of happiness will help you learn how to be happy right now. That has to be your goal, to be happy *now*. That has to be the goal for all of us, not money, not success, not the right love or the right looks. The goal has to be pure happiness.

Together, with this book, we will unlock the secrets of what it takes to lead happy lives, and as we move along through the chapters, I know you will indeed see your life improve.

Chapter One
The Pursuit of Happiness:
What Are You Seeking?

We all search for different things. Some of us seek money, some seek fame, some seek love, and some seek health. However, I believe that what we are all ultimately searching for is happiness. "I'll be happy if I find the love of my life . . . I'll be happy if I get that promotion and can purchase that car . . . I'll be happy if everyone knows my name . . . I'll be happy if my sickness is healed . . ." The list goes on. We seem to forget that people who have love, money, fame, or health are not necessarily happy.

Instead of those things that may or may not lead to happiness, we are going to examine what does give us long-lasting happiness.

First, you should know a little about me. From a very young age, I have passionately pursued happiness, exploring what makes us happy and how exactly we can be happy. My journey has been long and arduous, but along the way, I have gained some important insights into the art of being happy, staying happy, and maintaining happiness throughout one's life. And because I love to tell stories, I'll be sharing plenty of anecdotes to help you learn how to do the same. I believe this is why God put me here—to impart this knowledge and help others.

I absolutely guarantee that anyone, absolutely anyone, can be happy if he or she just works at it. At our core, happiness is the thing we are all pursuing. We may be searching for it by fanatically following our favorite sports team every weekend, by searching for love in the local clubs, or by toiling daily at work, hoping to make enough money so that all will be well. In the space of this book, we will explore these different paths and find out what truly helps us to be happy, stay happy, and live a happy life.

The following story explains what happiness, at its core, is all about.

*

There once was a man named Jim who constantly prayed to God for this and that, always wanting something. He prayed for more money, he prayed for true love, he prayed for his illness to be cured and his pain to disappear, and so on.

Late one night while Jim was saying his prayers, a voice began speaking to him out of nowhere. Although he felt very frightened, he finally mustered up the courage to ask, "Who is it?"

The voice answered, "I am God."

As you can imagine, Jim was both very scared and very excited. He asked God, "Why are you here, God? What do you want?"

God replied, "Jim, you have been praying to me for many, many years, constantly asking me for this and that. I have decided that I am going to give you one last thing. It can be anything you wish. However, what you ask for will be the last thing that I ever give you, so consider carefully what you want."

Jim was thrilled but extremely nervous. He really didn't know what to ask for and shuddered at the thought of making an unwise choice. So, he began asking his friends for advice.

One friend advised, "Ask for money!" but a second friend warned, "No! We all know people who have lots of money but who still have lots of problems." A third friend recommended, "Ask for a long life!" but yet another friend warned, "No! If you ask for that, you will outlive all your friends and loved ones, and you will be sad and lonely later in life."

Jim continued to question anyone and everyone what he should ask God for, but nothing seemed right. Every idea that anyone suggested seemed to have some type of downside, making it a bad choice.

Six months later, God came to Jim again. God said, "Jim, it has been six months, and I must have your answer. What is it that you want from me?"

Jim replied, "God, may I ask you a question first?"

God smiled and responded, "Yes, Jim, of course you may ask me a question. What is it?"

And so Jim asked, "God, can you tell me what to wish for? I don't know what I want."

Pleased with Jim's wisdom, God said, "Yes, Jim, I will tell you what to ask for. Jim, what you should ask for is to be content with whatever happens in your life."

Jim grinned and nodded, finally understanding what God was trying to teach him.

*

At its core, Jim's story tells us that if we learn to be content with what we have, then we are happy. If we learn to love what life has given us, then we are happy. Yes, we might desire to make a few changes here and there, and yes, everything might not go exactly the way we initially planned. However, if we celebrate and love what we have while at the same time working toward making changes, we will lead a happy life.

Think about those words: "be content with what we have." What does this mean for any of us? You might say, "I am in a job I don't like. Can I be happy?" Of course! Make adjustments as best you can, but if your job satisfaction still doesn't change, learn to be content with what you have. If you never seem to have enough money, then retrain your thinking and learn to be happy with what you have.

A scientific rule, which I reference frequently, states, "If any person in the universe can be happy with this situation, then happiness is a possibility for anyone." In other words, if someone has cancer but is happy, it means that any of us, even if we suffer from a similar misfortune, can be happy. If someone has lost the love of his or her life but is still able to find happiness, then anyone can find happiness. Later in the book, I will elaborate much further on this idea.

I am aware that this chapter may actually inspire more questions than answers. However, stick with me, and you will find your doubts addressed. Any of us can be happy, and I want nothing more than for you to keep exploring the world of happiness with me. Happiness isn't necessarily complicated, but it does take work. Together, let's explore how to be happy right now!

Chapter Two
Learning How to Live Life to the Fullest: Happiness and Chocolate . . .
Are They Similar?

I love chocolate! Although I try to eat a proper diet most of the time, I have definitely cultivated a taste for the sweet stuff. Thankfully, I have found a "healthier" version of chocolate that I really enjoy. I limit how often I treat myself, and I try to limit myself to this particular "healthier" kind of chocolate.

In the past, I was definitely much more indulgent in chocolate in its many forms. Many years ago when I was shopping at Costco, I found the most delicious, moist chocolate cake. And it was gigantic! The first bite was so exquisite I couldn't help taking another and another and yet another. But, after a few bites, it wasn't quite as good. Don't get me wrong; the cake was excellent, but each progressive bite wasn't quite as good as the experience of that first bite. And because the cake was so big, there was no way I could eat the entire thing in one sitting, so it lasted for quite a while. After a few days, I was pretty tired of that cake. By now you're probably wondering, "What does chocolate cake have to do with happiness?" My answer to you is "Quite a bit!" Let me explain.

Studies have shown that when we get something that is new and wonderful, eventually we get used to it, and after a while, most of these wonderful feelings get less intense. This is true of everything— a new car, new job, favorite ice cream, sitting on the beach after weeks of work—as well as those bites of chocolate cake. When we get used to something, when the newness of it has worn off, we stop enjoying it as much.

One of the key factors of happiness is keeping things new and not getting into a rut. Then, we will enjoy life a lot more. But how do we do this? How do we keep our hearts and minds new, fresh, and alive? It is not so difficult. Let's explore this together.

First, we must remember that it is nothing but our own mind that keeps us from viewing things as new and fresh. We tend to label or categorize things, and when we do so, we stop truly seeing them.

There is a wise old saying that goes, "Once I see a sparrow and name it, I stop seeing it." Once we have set expectations about something, we stop seeing it. The same principle applies to our experiences. Once we have a great experience—and usually we perceive this initial experience to be the most intense—we relate everything back to it and seek the same high again. But life doesn't always give us the same high again, particularly if we compare and contrast our experiences. It is this constant comparing and contrasting that keeps us from enjoying things in the present, right here and right now, and from feeling fresh, new, and alive with a wonderful richness and fullness beyond imagination.

There is a fun way we can experiment with this idea. Let me use my own experience as an example. On one Father's Day, I went with my children to the Getty Center, one of the most beautiful museums in the world. When I was there, some exquisite artwork was on exhibit, and I viewed it as I usually do. When I look at artwork, I first read the plaque and the artist's name, but then I just stand back and take in the colors, forms, and shapes. I don't label anything; instead, I simply open up my heart and, in a sense, feel the painting in a visual, more intuitive way. By letting my experience cogitate inside me at an emotional level, my emotions affect an outward expression.

Try this when you next see a work of art you would otherwise dismiss. Just stand back and, without judgment, look at it. Let your eyes move comfortably around the piece, see if you can feel what the artist was trying to convey, and let the work tell you its story. This is a wonderful way to interact with art. Actually, it is a wonderful way to interact with life!

Yes, sometimes we do need labels. Labels are important in remembering the past and particularly in identifying dangerous things.

However, we miss out on so much of life when we're wrapped up in our own notions of how things should be or look or behave, instead of just experiencing what is before us.

I have a special way of helping people get beyond the comfort of labels. At retreats I hold and other presentations, I bring high-quality, dark chocolate to share with everyone. Before we sample the treat, I say, "Let's pretend we are all aliens and have never seen this substance before. First, let's smell it and touch it and see what it's like. Then, if we think it's safe, let's put it to our lips and see if we have any adverse reaction. Then, let's put it to our tongues, still seeing if anything happens. What does it taste like? Then let's put a piece—not too big—into our mouths and hold it there without chewing or swallowing. Just keep the chocolate there and see what happens." At the end of this exercise, the chocolate seems to be the most exquisite piece of candy we've ever had in our lives! If you don't believe me, try this exercise yourself.

Now, this chocolate is high quality, but that has nothing to do with how we react to it. Instead, it seems to be the best chocolate in the world because we are experiencing it with all-new senses—fresh eyes and taste buds and smells. This exercise applies across the board, to everything in life. If we learn to quiet our minds and just be present with what is, then we learn to experience all the beauty and freshness of the world in a new, pristine state.

When we label, we don't see this nearly as well. We must realize and constantly remember that we tend to over-analyze. Our minds are going and going all day long, and we must learn how to still them and simply to enjoy life as it is right here, right now. It is all just about being aware. Once we are aware of how much we label, we'll start labeling less.

I love going on walks and listening to the birds and seeing the fresh flowers. Because I don't label them, I notice them each time as something new and wonderful. Life can be a wonderful adventure if we quiet our minds, stop labeling, and just enjoy the wonderful journey. If we see everything around us as new, we will enjoy life better and our experiences will be more intense, richer, and fuller. Even things we are used to seeing all the time will be better because we will see them with new eyes. All the details, large and small, will be enhanced.

It requires work and effort to create this way of thinking, but if we put forth the effort, we can successfully achieve this new way of perceiving and living. Once we stop labeling things and get out of our heads and just be, the entire, beautiful universe opens up to us.

Then, we will reap the benefits, finally aware of all the richness in life that has always been there but constantly overlooked.

Learn not to label things and, instead, see everything in this world as new and exciting. You will truly be amazed!

Chapter Three
The Importance of
Being Earnest to Be Happy

Are there only certain people that can be happy? In other words, is happiness limited to only a select few?

The great news is that any one of us can be happy, no matter our circumstances. It doesn't matter what we start out with in this world; we all can end up living a happy and joyful life. However, there is one thing that we need in order to achieve this—a principle that works across the board in life in general and with happiness especially: success.

What is needed to succeed? In my private practice in Newport Beach, California, one of the most exclusive zip codes in the world, I see the answer to this question all the time. The people I work with in Newport Beach are all very successful at what they do. What is the key, unifying ingredient that I see when working with these people? It is that they work hard and are earnest about being successful. They want to be successful, they learn from their mistakes, and they keep going forward.

A lot of people work hard but aren't necessarily successful. It's not just about hard work; it's also about working smart. Teachers, for example, can work really hard but aren't necessarily recognized for their efforts. But, if a teacher develops her skills, learns from her mistakes, moves forward, and keeps improving, she may end up being recognized as Teacher of the Year. That teacher worked smart.

Interestingly, once you are successful at something, you tend to breed success, seeing it return to you again. For example, in 2011, we were mired in a pretty rough recession. My clients in Newport Beach felt the effects of the bad economy, but because they're very gifted professionally, they adapted to the changes, moved forward, and continued to be successful.

As long as what you are pursuing is realistic, you can do it. However, if you want to achieve something outside the probable, such as become an Olympic athlete when you are past your prime and lack coordination, for example, this may not be feasible.

Achieving something like this is possible, but you need more than hard work and earnestness. You also need the right physical attributes, special talents, and special circumstances. Since there's a limited pool of people with the right combination of these factors, not everyone can achieve something specific like this.

But any of us can achieve general accomplishments, such as financial success, as long as we can adapt, learn, and grow. We can be very successful in many things in life as long as we apply this method. Any of us can be good at something if we apply the same skills of success.

When we pursue things like money, fame, success, or prestige, we are actually pursuing the deepest level of happiness. We all just want to be happy. That is the truth. Unfortunately, when we get on this path toward success, we think that if we reach our goals we'll be happy. But reaching these end goals doesn't automatically make us happy. When we reach our goals, we might say, "Wow! That actually didn't make me as happy as I thought. Everyone loves me, I have a lot of money, but I'm not truly happy."

We must remember that anything we can achieve can be taken away, even if we're fantastically successful and a multi-billionaire. Our achievements are inherently impermanent, and this threat of losing them always lurks. Life brings change. When change hits, we often suffer. If we want to be happy, we have to be very earnest about success and we have to work very hard. We must also be honest and be flexible. For example, if we run a business and it collapses or doesn't make us any money or doesn't bring us joy, we must take appropriate action—close it down and move on to something else. Only then will we be truly happy.

Unfortunately, when it comes to happiness, we often delude ourselves through addiction. We think what we are aiming for— money, fame, love, whatever—is our key to happiness. But once we achieve it and the intensity of happiness quickly wears off, we then think we need more of the same to get that feeling back. We keep going, looking for that high, saying, "I'm happy when I'm on my drug, so don't take my drug away." But since it can be taken away, obviously addictions don't work, and they cause us suffering.

Let me offer a different example. Perhaps we say to ourselves, "Right now, I really like what I'm doing. I'm in a loving relationship, and I have a couple of great kids. But sometimes I have these intense fears that kick in. I get very afraid when I hear stories about divorce, people losing their jobs, or someone's kids getting sick or being in a serious accident." If there is a threat to what we have right now, then ultimately we're really not completely happy. True contentment must be unconditional and available 100 percent of the time for us to be truly happy. If our happiness depends upon certain circumstances, then it's not really a true, lasting happiness.

Here's an example you can probably understand. Many years ago when my children were very young, three children were killed in a car accident in Orange County. After the accident, moms in the area were fearful because of what had happened, imagining losing their kids like that. It was such a dark, scary thing, and they suffered in thinking about what could happen. Even though their own children were very happy and doing well, just the fear of such a tragic incident caused the mothers unhappiness.

We must be honest when these bumps in life come, and we must deal with them, address them, feel them, and heal. Are we ultimately in a constant state of happiness? If we answer no, then this is where earnestness comes in. We must keep learning tools and skills that help us maintain and improve our constant state of happiness. It is possible for life to go very, very well, but it takes work. As long as we're not turning towards addictions, then we can find this constant state of happiness with earnestness. In turning towards addictions, people delude themselves into thinking they're happy when they're really not. We have to be honest, and addictions don't allow us to be honest. When we're truly feeling what we feel and we're honest, then we're going to keep working on finding ways to be in a regular state of happiness.

If we are rich or famous but unhappy, then we'll probably not enjoy life, even though outwardly we may seem successful. We must realize that we should strive to be happy now, even though we are still on our journey toward whatever we may be pursuing; the end result of our journey must not be the factor in our happiness. I believe any of us can have a very happy life right now. It takes work and honesty, but it's worth the effort.

Chapter Four
Waking Up at Princeton:
It's Not Always the Degree You Get
That Makes You Smart

Many years ago, when I was working toward my first master's degree at Princeton, I had an experience that changed my life and put me on a new path on how to live. I had accomplished much at Princeton: I was graduating with honors, I had won many awards for my research work, and I had been accepted into one of the top PhD clinical psychology programs in the United States. All seemed to be going well. But . . .

On a beautiful spring day, one of my last at Princeton, I decided to go to a park and just hang out for a few hours. The day was pristine, and I lay on my back on the grass, just gazing up at the sky and the trees. This moment spent lying on the lawn was the most beautiful experience I'd had during my entire stay at Princeton.

But the enjoyment turned bittersweet as I realized that, although I had been at the university for almost three years, I had never done this and I had missed out on just being: being present and enjoying nature and my surroundings. I had been so busy achieving that I had never paused to enjoy the simple wonders of the campus. It was a very sad experience for me but one that pushed me forward and helped me to start changing the way I lived my life. Of course, I didn't undergo an overnight change, but I did begin to slow down and enjoy the journey. Besides achieving, I started enjoying the process of moving forward, growing, and just being. I began to appreciate nature and life as it happens right here, right now.

When I moved to California upon graduating from Princeton, I discovered beautiful hiking trails, and I found many people in my doctoral program that would join me on different days for long walks. I was truly committed to take the time to enjoy life, instead of only focusing on achieving. And I wasn't alone. When I started exploring the trails, I probably had about ten people from my doctoral program who would hike with me at different times, on different days. It was so beautiful hiking on the hills and the mountains. Yet at the end of the program, I couldn't find one fellow student who had the time to go hiking anymore. Instead, I had to find other people who would join me; these people had obviously learned to enjoy the journey of life.

One of the key factors of happiness is that we do need to enjoy the journey, no matter what is happening in our lives. If we are on that achievement track, if we are trying to make money, earn a degree, achieve fame, etc., we still need to enjoy life along the way. It isn't that it is wrong to achieve, but it's wrong to miss out on life as we achieve. The path of achievement-driven gratification leads to a very empty, sad life.

Take pleasure in life, get out, be with friends, and embrace nature. It is important to enjoy the journey, to enjoy life as we achieve; we can do both. We have a tendency to cause our achievements and our goals to supersede living and loving life right here, right now. Often we say, "Someday I'll slow down. Someday I'll enjoy life, but right now, I need to achieve. I need to make it so I have time to slow down when I reach my goals. When I do reach my goals, then I'll slow down and enjoy life."

But why not achieve while slowing down a bit to enjoy the journey? We may reach our goals a little bit later, but we will be in much better shape if we take time for happiness along the way. And if life doesn't turn out the way we expected, it won't bother us as much because we had all that pleasure while working for the end. It's a win/win situation! We work towards our goals AND enjoy our journey.

Ultimately, what helps us is our passion. We must love our goals simply because we like working towards them. So even if we do not reach our goals, we will have loved what we were doing all along. If our goals don't work out, well, then we will just move on to the next dream and the next satisfying journey.

Chapter Five
Winning the Bronze Medal in Life:
What My Kindergartener Can Teach Us

Many of us put a lot of pressure on ourselves to achieve. When we don't live up to our expectations, we are often very hard on ourselves. Furthermore, we have an incredible tendency to compare ourselves to other people. If we don't live up to these imaginary determinants of success that we have created in our heads, we suffer.

I want to offer an alternative to this suffering, a lesson we can all learn courtesy of my six-year-old daughter.

Recently at her school, an awards ceremony was held to recognize reading achievement. Usually, the younger children all receive awards while the older children compete against one another for gold, silver, and bronze medals. Our children had attended this school for quite some time, and my son had won a gold medal every year. This year, for some reason, they decided that the kindergarteners should be competitive too.

It had been decided that the competition between kindergarteners would be based upon the number of sheets of paper they turned in throughout the school year, each sheet of paper representing one book. Now, my daughter loves books and loves to read. Unfortunately, I was unaware of this new rule, and although my daughter had definitely read enough books to qualify for a gold medal, I hadn't turned in papers for all the books she had read.

When I arrived at the ceremony, I realized that my daughter was one of the few kindergarteners to receive a bronze medal. Apparently, most of the other parents had caught on to the competition's new rules. In fact, almost all the kids were gold medalists! Now, I didn't care which medal my daughter received because I know she loves reading and school, and that's what is important to me. But I watched my daughter closely in order to gauge her reaction. Because she is in kindergarten and still quite young, she was so excited when she got her bronze medal, oblivious to the distinction of the different medals. When she sat down, she showed all her friends, smiling brightly. When her friends all came back with their silver and gold medals, my daughter was just as excited and happy. She wasn't comparing herself against the other kindergarteners and, instead, was excited about her own accomplishment and happy for theirs.

There is a lesson here for all of us. In life, the second we start comparing ourselves to other people, there is a potential for us to suffer. We must remember that we won't always win gold medals—in fact, few of us will. We will all occasionally experience failure, and we will all have setbacks. If we constantly compare ourselves to other people, we will experience constant suffering. No matter how successful we are, there will always be someone who is more successful.

Let me give you another example, this among adults. I work with people who have two, sometimes three homes. If these people have a beautiful home on the beach, they don't compare their home to ones like yours and mine, but instead, they compare it to the other beach homes. Or they compare themselves having only two homes to those who have three homes. We must remember that if we compare ourselves to other people, we are going to suffer for we will never out-match everyone. To be happy, we must stop doing this!

The great wisdom we can gain from my daughter is that she wasn't comparing herself to others. Instead, she was excited about her own individual accomplishment and celebrated her excitement. We can do the same; any of us can!

Suppose, for example, upon graduating from high school, you didn't pursue further education. Many people choose this route, and that's okay. There is absolutely no need to compare ourselves to others who possess a college degree while we have none, or who possess a master's degree while we only have a bachelor's degree, etc. Instead, let's celebrate what we DO have. Let's celebrate our children, our jobs, our friends, our memories, our lives! All we have to do is focus on what we DO have in our life and live it to the fullest. In doing so, we will lead a beautiful life because we will truly realize that every life is beautiful. However, the second we start comparing our lives to those of others, we will start suffering.

Let us remember that even if we win today, tomorrow we may lose. It is much better not to play the comparison game and, instead, celebrate our own lives as they are. Experiencing joy in what we do have is a better way to live and is one of the key components of happiness.

To stop playing the comparison game, we need to do two things. First, we have to accept the fact that comparing ourselves to others isn't good for us and will cause suffering. Sooner or later, we are going to lose. Wouldn't it be better to do something for the love of it, not caring if we win or lose? It is not that we can't still be competitive, but if we lose, we should keep a smile on our face and say, "Hey, I had a great time doing that whether I won or lost." As long as we need our self-esteem to be validated externally, we will suffer. We play the comparison game because we want others to think highly of us. We must remember that no matter how highly others think of us, their opinions are not going to make any difference.

It is not hard to prove this. Think of all the successful or famous people in this world. Are they always happier than a regular Joe? Always? No. And often not even some of the time. Successful or famous people still commit suicide and still do destructive things to themselves and to their careers. If it were true that being the best or being on top will make you happier, then all the successful or famous people should be happy all the time. But they're not. How many times do we witness people who are at the peak in their profession leading a path of self-destruction? Being a CEO, a famous movie star, or top athlete isn't necessarily the way to find happiness. It is far better to do what we love just for the love of it and to enjoy life as we are living it. When we are passionate about what we're doing and we're unconcerned about what others think of us, then we are happy. We must remember that the game of success can change in a heartbeat.

If you believe, as I do, that constantly comparing our achievements is not good for us, then what do we do? How do we make sure we don't fall into that trap? The key is awareness. We are conditioned at a very young age to compare ourselves to others. Recall the early conditioning taking place in my daughter's kindergarten class where the school changed how medals were awarded. We must un-condition or recondition ourselves. The way we can accomplish this is through awareness. Throughout the day, we need to be mindful and watch our thoughts, observing how often we compare ourselves to other people. *Is she more beautiful? Does he have a nicer car? Do they have a nicer home?* These types of thoughts and comparisons go on and on.

If we become aware of our thoughts, then we can change them. For example, let's say we are driving our car and perhaps a nicer car drives by. We can look at that nicer car, feeling envious and saying things like, "Oh, they have a nicer car! Wow! They must have more money," and so on. But instead, if we distract our thoughts and do something else besides making a comparison, then this constant comparing will happen less often.

We must also be careful of people who indulge in this comparison game. Some play it for keeps. These people look down on others because of what they perceive to be the others' failures and are always talking about other people or their own successes. We do not need to hang around these people. They addicted to winning the comparison game. Would we want to have such addicts as friends? Probably not. People can get so caught up in always trying to be better than someone else. This way of living is purely self-destructive because the person will never be good enough.

One of my very close friends drives an old truck, even though he does well financially. He is extremely unpretentious, and that's why he is one of my good friends. I have others that also don't play the comparison game. If you find yourself surrounded by people who are playing the game, just change the subject and walk away. You will find that once you become more aware of it, you'll participate less, and life will become much easier and will flow much better.

So like my daughter, let's celebrate the bronze medals we get in life as joyfully as the gold medals. Just living is worth celebrating! If we manage to do that, then we will find that we are much happier and will enjoy life so much more.

Chapter Six
The Road to Happiness Is Found by Focusing on What We Have

Our minds create many thoughts that can lead to our being unhappy. But, the key phrase here is "our minds create." The thoughts and beliefs that we hold in our minds greatly impact everything about us.

Here in the United States and in most places in the developed world, people are consumed by consumerism. So much of our unhappiness comes from wishing that things were different, wishing that we had something else instead of what we do have.

I met a woman once who had a beautiful daughter. Although very happy with her daughter, the mother really wanted another child. Even though her husband loved her and her daughter loved her, the woman was so utterly unhappy because she didn't have a second child. All her mental energy, all her mental commentary, went towards that focus, and because of that, she suffered greatly.

To those of us not in this woman's situation, we may think her attitude unfortunate or odd, but that story holds a lesson I hope encourages all of us to spend some time, maybe even stop at this very moment, to reflect upon: "In my own life, what am I focused on that I don't have?" I can guarantee that if we focus on what we don't have, we're going to be unhappy and we're going to suffer. Our unhappiness can stem from anything that we're focusing on. Maybe we think we'll be happy when we lose those extra fifty pounds. Maybe happiness will come when we reach a certain financial level or get that promotion. Maybe we'll finally be happy when we meet our soul mate and begin a new life together. Or maybe, as in the example of the woman with only one daughter, we think when we have a child, then we'll finally be happy. The list can become endless because, the second that we fulfill one of our desires, a new one takes its place, and so we just continue to suffer.

In many ways, our lives are like that of King Sisyphus from Greek mythology. He was sentenced to the eternal punishment of rolling a large boulder up a hill. Every time he pushed it to the top, the boulder would roll back down, and he would have to start all over again; it never ended for him. I think sometimes our minds are like that; they just don't stop wanting. No matter what we desire or wish for, at any age, something else will come along very quickly, and we'll say, "Now I want that." It's almost shocking if you think about it, and it can continue throughout our lives. Young children just can't wait to get presents on their birthdays or at Christmas. But quickly, often shockingly fast, they tire of their new toys and go on to something else. Does this ever change? As we get older, we our new toys become bigger and grander, like a new car, a new spouse, a new home, and yet we tire of them quickly and move on. We want something different, something more. We're unhappy with what we have, and we're always yearning after something different.

So how do we get off this continuous and debilitating wheel of suffering? Is there any freedom from our Sisyphean task of living our lives? Yes, there is, and it's actually shockingly simple. All we have to do is be happy with what we have. Again, this is so important I want you to hear that again:

All we have to do is be happy and be focused on what we have right here, right now.

But how do we do this in our daily life when our minds very quickly return to thinking about what we don't have? First, we must realize this type of focusing is not going to help us. We have to believe that focusing on what we don't have is going to cause us suffering. And we must believe that concentrating on what we do have and are blessed with right now is going to put a smile on our faces. In many ways, this is as powerful as $E = MC^2$ and just as beautiful and simple. All we have to do is be happy with what we have and not think about what we don't have. It's that simple yet also elegant and beautiful.

As we think about this, we have to realize that this changed philosophy of ours isn't going to make the consumer marketers and advertisers of the world very happy. They spend billions of dollars trying to get us to be unhappy with how things are now—so we'll feel "less than"—and we'll want something different. Otherwise, we're not going to spend money to buy what they're selling.

I don't blame only the marketers and advertisers for our continual wanting. We're as guilty as they are. We do the same thing to ourselves by thinking about what other people have, such as success or love or whatever it may be. And because we're thinking about what they have and what we don't have, we become unhappy. Instead, what if we focused on what we had? What if we focused on the beautiful things that we have in our lives? Some of us may have less than others, but we ALL can still have a beautiful life.

Even those who have very little can be happy. I've seen this when I've spent time at monasteries and gotten to know many who live there. When you choose to live a monastic life, you give up just about everything, and I do mean pretty much everything. Yet these people who live such simple lives are often the happiest people I have ever met. They can have virtually nothing in the form of material possessions, and they can still focus on what they do have—a love of life right here, right now—and they're happy.

So why can't we do the same? Why can't we focus on what we do have? We can!

We might not have the nicest house in the neighborhood, but maybe we have a beautiful family living in that house. Maybe we don't feel very well physically sometimes, but we are free and able to go for lots of walks in nature, and we can enjoy being outside. Maybe we haven't yet found the love of our life, but we have awesome friends who care about us and spend time with us. The list of what we do have can go on for a long time if we start focusing on exactly that, what we do have, and celebrate it.

Thinking about what we do have and appreciating it as we engage with it makes all the difference in gaining that elusive happiness, This doesn't have to involve a lot of effort. Just going for a walk in the early morning when everything is peaceful and still can bring us happiness beyond our wildest imagination. Being with friends, connecting with them, and loving them can be more satisfying than staying at the most expensive, grand hotel in the world. The list of what we do have and can focus on goes on and on. By proactively realizing that we need to focus on what we have and stop focusing on what we don't have, we'll discover one of the key secrets of happiness: We gain happiness right here, right now by focusing on what we have.

Be happy with what we have and stop focusing on what we don't have. Once we do this, then we can live a beautiful, happy, fulfilled life.

Chapter Seven
Where Are the Hippies and How Is the Media Powerful?

In the 1960s, our world became wealthier and in response, the hippie movement came about. It said that wealth may be fine but too much wealth isn't good for us, so we need to go against that wealth, spend time in nature, find peace and happiness in what's here right now, and not be so caught up into the wealth addiction because money isn't going to make us happy. We needed to find that wealth isn't the solution to everything and won't necessarily make us happy. We can find happiness in other things besides money.

Now, we're living in another wealth explosion, another wealth addiction. Many people are addicted to the acquisition of wealth right now, thinking that if they're wealthy enough they're going to be happy. So why isn't there a hippie movement again? Why isn't there a large part of our culture going against this wealth addiction?

The answers are very important for those of us seeking happiness in this life right now.

Here is the big difference: In the 1960s, we had television, but it wasn't as powerful as it is today. There were only three main television stations, and companies hadn't become that sophisticated in marketing through through this medium. In the twenty-first century, all that has changed. Marketers are pros at using television, and what they've brainwashed us and taught us to believe we need things to be happy. Added to this, they say, the more things we have, the happier we're going to be.

Brainwashing works. Think about it as a tool that marketers use to get us to buy things they want to sell to us. It works on all people, even—or especially—children. Around Christmas time, marketers run commercials for new toys. The kids will see those ads and tell their parents they really, really, really, *really* want the new toys. The parents buy, the children get, and the companies sell. The marketing and brainwashing work.

We are not any different from those children. We too are impacted by all the marketing to which we are exposed. We too want those things. We too have been brainwashed. And that's why I believe there hasn't been a hippie movement against this wealth addiction that we are facing today: We've bought in. The less-wealthy people are frustrated with the wealthy but actually want to be wealthy themselves. They're wishing they could be richer, and because they're not, they're not happy.

People have been brainwashed into thinking that wealth works. They think they will be happy if they're wealthy. Most people realize this is not true, but their actions in how they respond to life show the opposite. So they are unhappy because they're not wealthy, and the people that are wealthy are unhappy because the money doesn't buy happiness for them either.

All this brainwashing is about the power of ideas and thoughts. They matter. These ideas and thoughts can affect our whole world, and clearly they're powerful. So what we need to do is ask ourselves, "If thoughts matter, if ideas that I expose myself to matter, what am I exposing myself to?" Everything to which we are exposed matters. Everything. What I watch on television, what I read, whom I talk to, but most important what I am thinking about all day long all matter tremendously. What you think about all day long results from what you expose yourself to. It's a catch-22. What you watch affects what you think, and what you think affects how you see the world. So we need to make the choice to be happy. Whatever ideas are formulating in our lives are going to affect us, either in a good or bad way. If we're listening to the Happiness Podcasts, we're exposing ourselves to good ideas, but if we're watching or listening to negative, critical reports or advertising that feeds the wealth addiction, that is what we're going to get. Whatever we expose ourselves to will impact us.

I've seen the positive results of this in my travels around the world where I've sought out the healthiest people I could find. Over the years, I have found that the people who are the healthiest are also the happiest people I've ever met. And I can tell they are very careful about what they expose themselves to in all aspects of life. They expose themselves to positive, good things.

What we take in from the world around us is a lot like the food we eat. If we eat well, we're going to have good results; if we eat candy or consume alcohol or things that are not good for us, we're going to have different results. If we eat well, we will feel well; it we eat poorly, we will feel poorly. Everything matters, *everything*. Desserts are okay in moderation. If we eat dessert all the time, it's bad for us. The same goes for alcohol. A little bit of alcohol once in a while is not a big deal. Drink a lot of it, however, and you can become an alcoholic.

The same is true with our thoughts. If we're watching and exposing ourselves to things that are beautiful, that are positive, that really feed our happiness, then that's what we're going to get—beautiful, positive thoughts and happiness. Once in a while, being involved with something that isn't absolutely healthy is okay because it's not in large amounts. But what I'm talking about is 90 to 95 percent of what we expose ourselves to. If it feeds our happiness and helps us move in the direction of being happy, we are going to be happy.

So we have to ask ourselves what are we feeding our minds in regards to happiness? Are we having conversations that are negative to other people or ourselves? Or are we talking only of the good others do and accepting people with their imperfections? Are we watching shows that are critical or harsh? Or are they beautiful and wonderful? Are the people in our lives critical, harsh, and negative? Or are they supportive, loving, and kind? It all matters. We can't totally isolate ourselves from everything, but we can choose much of what comes into our lives, and the more selective we are and the more careful about what goes into our minds, the better we will do in life.

As an example, I have worked with a few people over the years that have struggled with depression. Like many people, they were watching a lot of the news. When they stopped, their negativity, depression, and anxiety abated; they got better. We are affected by everything we expose ourselves to. Mostly, it's our thoughts that we have in our heads, but everything else around us affects those thoughts. We have to ask ourselves, is it good for us?

Now, we don't want to be overwhelmed by totally changing our lifestyle. It's like if you've been overdoing the consumption of sweets and then all of a sudden you eat only fruits and vegetables.

The change can be so challenging you'll quickly revert to refined sugar. But if we start small, we're more likely to succeed in the long run. For instance, we can seek out people that are more positive and spend time with people who are uplifting and loving. Over time, we're going to get used to that.

The difficult part is that former ways—whether sugar and alcohol or negative friends we're used to—can be thrilling and making the change to healthier choices feel boring. But if you truly want to find happiness that surpasses everything you can imagine, you have to move in the direction of watching everything you're exposing yourself to and you'll see that what seems bland to other people's taste is wonderful to those who are healthy and happy. They don't need the thrills of wealth, materialism, drugs, or alcohol. Instead, just watching a beautiful sunset, spending time with someone you love, being in nature, and so on can be achieved any time and make you happy. It doesn't require anything of you, and it's so freeing to be happy without all the stuff, the negativity, and the downside that goes with materialism.

We can be happy, but it takes effort. We have to work at it and not assume we're going to be happy just because we want to be. After all, everyone wants happiness. That's why so many are pursuing things like wealth and addictions. But if we want to be happy, we have to pursue happiness, and that's an internal journey —happiness isn't external. Happiness comes when we are content with whatever is happening and find beauty and peacefulness in this contentment. Any of us can have it right now, but we have to work on finding it and be careful about influences that will be pushing us away from true, long-lasting happiness. They will try to teach us that if we have certain things, then we will be happy. Remember, these thoughts are incredibly powerful, thanks to the media's brainwashing that wealth addiction is a good thing. If a worldwide hippie movement can be repressed through the media, then clearly, what we expose ourselves to matters and we have to be careful, not in a fearful way but by an increased awareness of the influence of the media and all else around us.

So here are three steps you can take to make sure you're exposing yourself to good things.

First, be aware of what you are exposing yourself to. You can't change anything until you're aware.

Second, ask yourself if something is good or bad for you. Again, something bad once in a while is okay, but if it's happening all the time, then your whole life can start becoming negative.

Third, if you want to change for the better, then make the choice to give up bad things and bring in only good things that are healthy for your mind, feed your happiness, and don't take away from it. This could include bringing into your life people who are good for you. Start listening—really listening—to how things affect you. Do they put a smile on your face after you do it? Not just for the moment but permanently. For example, if I drink too much alcohol right now, I may feel better, but tomorrow morning, I'm going to feel horrible. In the long run, is what you're exposing yourself to good for you? Is it helping you be a happier person? If so, then do more of it. If it's negative, then do less.

These three steps—look at what you are doing, ask yourself if it is good or bad for you, and then start doing things that are good and doing less of the things that are bad for you—can give you a beautiful life. But we do need to acknowledge how powerful what we expose ourselves to is and how much it can impact us. Once we acknowledge it and really see it for what it is, then we will begin to move in the direction of making sure that everything we're exposing ourselves to is moving us in the direction of happiness.

The most important consideration in finding happiness is what we think about all day long. When we watch the commercial that is teaching us that wealth addiction is the way to happiness, we are reinforcing that idea. When we think that if we had certain things we'd be happy, we are strengthening that thought. Yes, things around us are powerful, but what is far more powerful is when we let brainwashing take hold and start reinforcing those ideas through our own thoughts.

We choose what we think and can encourage positive influences on our thoughts by, for instance, listening to my Happiness Podcast and finding ways to be happy. These are just as, if not more, powerful at creating change in us and brainwashing us in a good way. Why not brainwash towards happiness instead of towards desires and things that are never fulfilling?

It was a lesson that helped me in the most powerful way when I realized that, yes, everything matters but what if I exposed myself to very positive, loving, helpful things? I will become healthier and happier. It works. It's a law of nature. So let's choose that path of happiness. Let's choose to expose ourselves to things that fill us up and not empty us so that we can all have beautiful, happy lives.

Chapter Eight
You Deserve to Be Happy NOW!

You've seen all the tabloids at the grocery store's checkout, sensationally describing the lives of people all over the world and how some of them haven't turned out very well. These newspapers and magazines usually pick on famous people who have done some misdeed or who've had something go wrong in their lives, and the tabloid is trying to exploit it to sell papers. I don't think I've ever purchased one of those magazines because I think every person matters, even the rich and famous, and in their lives I'd love for them to be happy too; we all deserve to be happy. However, I do think these newspapers and magazines have something to teach us.

What almost everyone, and I do mean almost everyone, thinks in the pursuit of happiness is "When I obtain this, then I'll be happy." Often, this goal is in pursuit of a relationship, a new job, a certain amount of money, or great fame. Yet the lesson of the tabloids is that the famous people who have many of the things we say we want aren't happy themselves. But why? What's going on here?

We see this on a lesser level among our friends. For instance, when someone does well in business and now is very wealthy, we wonder, "But is he happy?" Or even with a classmate who fell in love and married his high school sweetheart, we ask, "But is he happy?" Are these people who got what they wanted happy? We wonder and in asking the question, we tend to lessen what they achieved by thinking they didn't find happiness. They reached an empty goal. This reasoning reinforces for us that these different things people achieve don't bring them happiness. Fame, money, success, love—friends as well as the famous may have these things, but it doesn't mean they're happy.

Interestingly, the reverse is also true. When we know someone is happy, it never occurs to us to ask, "Are they wealthy? Are they at the top of their field? Are they famous? Do they live in a beautiful home? Is their spouse gorgeous? Did their kids get into an ivy league school?" A person could be poor, uneducated, living alone, and not be very attractive, but still be happy. We all know people that are like that. And we envy them.

In my book, *Living a Peaceful Life,* I talk about a woman I know named Betty, who was physically in pain and very poor, her only child lived in a foreign country, and yet she was clearly one of the happiest people you could ever meet. She even described herself that way, as a very happy person.

What is going on here?

This is very simple: We don't need anything to be happy.

Nothing has to happen to make us happy. There are people out there who don't have anything and are extremely happy. Happiness stands alone. However, anything else doesn't.

The tabloids keep teaching us that people who are wealthy sometimes aren't happy. People that are famous sometimes aren't happy. Even people who are smart aren't necessarily happy. A doctor friend of mine told me his son got into Harvard and that Harvard students have a problem with depression. I think what happens there is that a student finally reaches the top of the academic world and then finds out that being there doesn't bring him the happiness he expected; so he struggles with depression.

Don't get me wrong. I'm not at all suggesting we should stop pursuing our goals. We just need to understand that reaching our goals may not, in and of itself, make us happy. When I work with young professionals, they sometimes tell me, "Well, when I get there, I'll feel differently. I'll be happy." But it's always the same: it doesn't work. Just reaching our goals isn't what is going to bring us happiness.

So what IS going to bring us happiness? What can we do instead? It's actually very simple. If happiness is what we pursue and only what we pursue and we have good direction, then we'll end up being happy. Other things won't get us to our happiness. So, we have to be careful about how much time and energy we give to these other pursuits.

Let me give you a clear example of how this works. In my work, I meet many professional people: medical doctors, psychologists, professors, researchers, lawyers, and others. What I've found along the way is that they spend a lot of time working on their goals of being a professional and reaching the top of their field. But, they don't spend much time enjoying themselves and being happy right now.

In my own case, I love sunsets. I live in southern California, and we have beautiful sunsets. Now, you're not likely to ask me if I'm happy because I'm watching a sunset. You're just going to see that I'm watching a sunset and that's making me happy. But when I talk to my professional colleagues, it's amazing how hard it is to get them to stop and watch sunsets. I often encourage them, but they resist. You know what the problem is? They know sunsets are awesome, but they're too busy pursuing their goals so that some later day they can watch sunsets. Really, that's basically what they do. They think, "Someday I'll be happy." I think, instead, "Why not be happy now?"

Life is replete with things we can do that will encourage us to be happy—spending time in nature, smelling a rose, watching an animal in the wild. These are things that, in and of themselves, are so astounding that it's hard for us not to be happy while we're enjoying and participating in them.

So, what we need to decide is, "I'm going to spend time just working on being happy." When that's our goal, because happiness stands alone and it doesn't need anything else, then guess what will happen? We'll end up being happy, right here, right now.

Chapter Nine
Living Today vs. "Someday I'll . . ."

The person who normally cuts my hair got sick, so I had to get a new hair stylist. I found Lisa, and her salon was right next to my office, so I went there and we started talking. It was quickly apparent that this woman loves what she does. The longer we talked, the more this was confirmed. Even as a young child, she wanted to cut hair. That's all she ever wanted to do—cut hair and eventually open her own salon, which she obviously did. She is absolutely passionate about what she does.

As she snipped and cut, she told me her mom had once told her that about 90 percent of people who go to work hate what they do, and they do it just because it's a job and what they have to do to make money. Lisa decided then and there, as a child, that she didn't want to be a part of that 90 percent. She chose to cut hair because she just really loves doing it.

Lisa's story is a good story for us to focus on because we hear so many people often say the opposite, "Someday I'll . . . live" or "Someday I'll . . . enjoy life." So many say things like, "I'll work hard right now, make lots of money, have lots of prestige, lots of fame [or whatever it may be], and then someday I'll enjoy life, someday I'll start living." Many people do this, and it's very sad because they're missing out on living life right here, right now.

This "someday" way of life doesn't bring us happiness mainly because we can never be sure that reaching our goal will bring us the happiness we assume it will. It might not. However, if we do what we love and we're passionate about it, whether we reach our goals or not, we're going to be happy all along the journey. Life and happiness are about enjoying the journey.

I'm not sure if Lisa's mom was right about the percentages. But I do think many people go to work just because they have to, or they're working hard right now so that someday they'll reap the rewards of all of their labor. The thing is, though, there just aren't any guarantees in life. We don't know how long we're going to live —we might never see that "someday." And even if we reach our goals, we don't know whether getting there will indeed make us happy. But if we do find happiness only after working hard to reach our goal, we still will have sacrificed having all that joy along the way—including time with those we love. That can have dire consequences on the relationships in our lives. Plus, chasing after tomorrow can cause a lot of health problems.

Let me share another story that illustrates my point. The person who normally cuts my hair, Ingrid, once told me about a couple who was so wealthy that they did everything to the nth degree. Ingrid knew them through her husband, who is a successful photographer. He took pictures for this couple's wedding, and they asked Ingrid and her husband to come along on the cruise afterward to photograph their honeymoon. While they were on this elaborate cruise, the newly married woman ordered Beluga caviar. She became so upset when she tasted it because she said it wasn't Beluga caviar and let this incident spoil the honeymoon for her. Obviously, having a lot of money doesn't necessarily bring happiness.

What does bring happiness is enjoying today, enjoying right now, enjoying the journey of our life. On the other hand, what can keep us from enjoying our life's journey is that little phrase, "Someday I'll be happy"—"Someday I'll be rich and then happy" or "Someday I'll be successful and happy" or "Someday I'll find the love of my life and be happy." It's not wrong to have goals and to work towards them. But our goals shouldn't keep us from living life and doing what we love right now. We can do both.

I know not everyone has an ideal job, but since we spend so much time doing work, there are ways we can enjoy it a little bit more. If we're a stay-at-home mom, let's do things that we enjoy and not make everything about sacrificing for our kids. If we go to a job that's laborious, one that's hard on us, let's find a way to enjoy it. Let's enjoy our lunches, let's enjoy the people we work with, and let's bring things that make our work better and more pleasant for us. Whatever we are doing, let's enjoy it to the fullest, instead of saying, "Someday I'll enjoy this."

None of us knows how long we have on Earth. There are absolutely no guarantees with life. Of course, we don't want to live so fully that we end up becoming homeless and not working. That would be silly. However, it's a matter of finding that balance. Let's enjoy what we do while we work. That's the key to whatever we're doing in life. The relationship we're in, can we make it better? The job that we do, can we improve it? A little bit of improvement over time can drastically affect our overall life. When we meet people like Lisa, who passionately love what they do, we realize that happiness isn't always about how much money they make. It's far more about doing what they love, loving what they do, and loving life. That's the secret of happiness—loving life now and not "someday."

I know that sometimes we're in very difficult situations in life. We may be in prison; we may be diagnosed with cancer; we may be unemployed. Many negative things that can happen to us. But even in those challenging times, there is always something beautiful to be with. Be with that something beautiful. Yes, work towards remedying the negative that's going on, but when we've done our part, then we need to relax and just enjoy what is. There's always something beautiful to be with; let's be with that.

Here are the key elements.

1. We just don't know how long we have to live, so let's not put off living fully today in the hope for a better tomorrow. Let's live today to the utmost.
2. Let's always realize that, no matter what's happening, there is always something beautiful to be with.

If we believe these two things, then we'll look for and find these beautiful things to be with right here, right now, even with the challenges we face in our everyday life. The important thing is to live now and stop waiting for "Someday I'll . . ."

"Someday I'll . . ." may never come. But if we enjoy the journey of our life and work towards our goals, what will happen is that, even if we don't reach them, we will have a good life.

Chapter Ten
Finding Happiness by Flowing with Life

Part of finding happiness in our lives means that we have to understand who we are, where we stand, what our nature is, what our interests and passions are, and then making these part of our lives.

For example, I love nature, I love being outside, but my work as a psychologist normally occurs inside. So when I get up in the morning, I go for a walk. Then on my way to work, I stop along the beach and go for a longer walk. Whenever I have breaks between clients, I go for another walk. You'll often see me outside enjoying nature. Life flows well for me and filters into the rest of my life when I'm in nature, when I'm outside. This can be walking in the neighborhood, along a park, or on the beach.

Unfortunately, I see many people don't flow with life. Rather, they fight life. They could be working towards some goal, academic or professional, and because they're working so hard towards it, they put aside their flow, their natural love and passions, in order to reach this goal. Others get caught up in some addiction—alcohol, drugs, or relationships—instead of doing things that are good for them. In both of these situations, we suffer because we're not flowing with life. We're not keeping our life simple and engaging in activities that fill us up.

Imagine for a moment that we're a beautiful flower. As long as we get the proper sunshine, healthy soil, and the right amount of good clean water we thrive. But when we're put in dark places or surrounded by contaminated dirt or deprived of nourishing water, we shrivel, suffer, and maybe die. A similar thing happens on a psychological level.

I remember once reading a study about children who were allowed to eat whatever they wanted from the choices given them, which did not include sugary foods. They naturally ate a balanced diet; the children knew intrinsically what their bodies needed. But they were not allowed to have any sugar because they would not have listened to their bodies and eaten a healthy meal.

As long as we take the time to figure out what our needs are, what fills us up and makes us happy (much as the flower is happy with sunshine, good soil, and clean water), then we will make sure we get them. We know what we need to remain balanced.

Happiness is really a very simple way to approach life. When instead we stock our life full of activities, television, things that distract us from our internal selves or with addictions like drugs, alcohol, work, constant busyness, then we don't really know what we need. The first step towards flowing naturally with life is to simplify our lives. We have to slow down and ask, "What do I need?"

By having moments of stillness, we often see what we need, which may not be constant over our lifetime. We need to remain open to learning of new needs as they can change in time. For example, for many years, I worked three long days and then took four days off. Later in my life, I realized it was time for me to change that schedule and work five normal days. Now, as I continue to get older, I've learned that my life flows much better when my activities and work are completed earlier and don't extend too late in the evenings. So now I'm in the process of slowing down my practice and not working as late. But I came to these discoveries by checking in every now and then to see how I was doing. If we don't take time to assess how we're doing in the flow of life, then we don't know what we need and likely won't get it.

What we really need to work towards is finding our flow right now when our lives aren't too full of activities. What do we need to make our day, our moments, go well? The answer is going to be very simple. Happiness has a flow to it that relates to who we are. For example, if someone is very passionate about the arts but is working in the medical field, then the person needs to find ways to make his or her work more artistic or change to a different field. Doing something for the sake of money or for making other people proud of us does not translate into our being happy. We create suffering and unhappiness for ourselves. We're not going to change this overnight. But by saying, "What naturally is good for me, fills me up, and puts a smile on my face?" starts us on the right path, working towards greater happiness.

For example, having an affair might feel good at the time, but all the pain and suffering it's going to cause isn't worth that moment of pleasure. It won't make us smile in the end. Instead, coming home, spending time with the people we love, letting them know how much we love them, and making time for these relationships that are important to us will have a flow to it. It's going to go well and make us happy.

Spending time in nature is a great way to get that flow in life because nature is simple, beautiful, and rejuvenating. It demands nothing of us but fills us up with positive feelings and a restful mood after we're in it. It helps us feel better. When we go on vacation, if it's a natural, relaxing vacation, we come back feeling refreshed, rejuvenated, and ready to continue our life of work and serving others.

Life goes best when we flow with it, even in the process of helping and caring for others. If we like something and it's important to us, we should make time to take part in it. For example, if we enjoy building things with our hands, we should take time out of our everyday lives and build something. An example could be working with Habitat for Humanity where we can build homes for people. If we hate working with money, then we probably shouldn't volunteer helping an organization keep its books. Spending our free time doing something we dislike is counterproductive to finding happiness and working in our flow.

A lot of life is working towards our flow. It's simple. We do things every day that are good for us and don't require a lot of strain or anxiety. It's about asking, "What works for me? What is just naturally good for my soul?" and listening closely to our honest answers. If we love gardening, then we have to make time to garden, and that should be a big part of our lives. If we love nature and animals, then we should be involved with them. Find what resonates with us, what satisfies us, what sparks our passion. What activity or interest adds to us and doesn't take away from us?

How do we discover what we love to do? An easy way to determine this is to ask, "After I do this activity, in the long term, do I feel better or do I feel worse?" We have to figure out what satisfies us in the end and not just in the fleeting moment. The short-lived pleasure ultimately causes us pain, and we want to avoid that. It could be something like coming home, unwinding with a couple of glasses of wine, and watching mindless shows on TV. Another example could be coffee every morning to get our day started.

We're looking for the flow that works best for us right now that we don't have to fight. If we're not a morning person, then we need to move in the direction of making our lives less dictated by mornings. Or if we're not an evening person, our days can wind down earlier. Again, we have to first figure out what works for us so we can find the best rhythm for our lives.

Once you have that answer then work in the direction of making these things happen. That can seem overwhelming at first, but here's a 5 percent rule that can be helpful. Just make a 5 percent improvement at a time, and soon enough, that 5 percent becomes 100 percent change. If we take on a monumental task, especially in changing ourselves, it overwhelms us, and we often quit before we've barely begun. But if we move in the right direction and do a little bit at a time, we make incremental changes and success. We see we are making a difference, feel internally rewarded, and continue making advances.

For example, we say, "Hey, I'm going to go to bed ten or fifteen minutes earlier at night by so I'll wake up in the morning a little bit more refreshed." Or perhaps we say, "I'm not ready to give up my two glasses of wine in the evening for a walk. Instead, I'll start walking on the weekends. I'll go around the neighborhood for a block or so, make that my normal routine, and then carry it over to the weekday." With little changes that you gradually increase, you will see that you will have moved into the direction of having some great self-care and flowing with life.

In flowing with life, we flow with happiness. This is an easy way to increase the things in our lives that are good for us. Know that they are simple things, like walking. By making room in our lives for these simple activities, we must say no to some other things, which are not enhancing our lives. Part of flowing with life is a simple life, one not cluttered with activity.

What I've done in my own life is to say no to things all the time. I am regularly invited to social events, give talks to groups, visit, be part of the media, and so on, but I say no to them quite often. I do this because I've learned that for my life to flow well I need time for walks. I excuse myself by simply saying, "I'm busy." And that is the truth. That busyness might be that I'm spending time with my kids. That busyness might be that I'm meditating. Or it might be that I'm walking the beach. People accept that simple "I'm busy," and in return, I can stay with my flow and remain happy.

You can do this too.

Flowing is good for us. We have to listen to our bodies, listen to our souls, and flow with life so that happiness can settle on our shoulders like a butterfly.

Chapter Eleven
Meditation:
The Path Away from Addiction

Why are addictions so powerful? Why do we turn to them? How we can turn away from them, as we must, because of the negative consequences they ultimately deal out?

Addictions come in all shapes and forms. We can all think of stories about people who are addicted to drugs and alcohol. These types of abuses are very common throughout the world. One of my uncles, with whom I grew up and of whom I was very fond, struggled with alcohol. He was a very giving, loving person, but the years of drinking alcohol truly destroyed his life. He was a very handsome, fun person to be around, and he used to train animals for Hollywood. One summer when I was a boy, he drove all the way to Iowa with a lion that he pulled in a trailer behind his car, stopping at our home for a visit. It was very exciting for me and formed a wonderful memory in my mind. But his daily use of alcohol shriveled his body, aged him, and cut his life short. Before he died, he lived by himself and had turned into a mean, unhappy man. My memories of him go back to his good years, but it's sad to think how his life and happiness were so cheated by his addiction to alcohol.

What are addictions? Addictions are basically emotional pain killers. When we have something inside us that is upsetting, disconcerting, and emotionally charged, we have two options. The first is to feel it, get over it, heal it, and get better. The second option is to stuff it, repress it, hold the feelings in, and keep it inside ourselves. Just as if I have a physical ailment such as a horrible cut, I can go to the doctor, get stitches, and heal it the proper way. If I instead just take painkillers, neglecting the cut itself, it won't hurt anymore, but it will only get worse, perhaps getting gangrene and possibly even killing me. Emotions work the same way, but slower. We need to feel our feelings, get over them, heal, and move on. It's pretty simple actually, but it's very hard for many of us to do. Why?

Again, the answer is simple. In the short term, addictions work; they take away the pain now. When you have to feel something, like that cut, it hurts at first. It can hurt quite a bit to clean it and take care of it properly. It can hurt quite a bit to clean out that emotional wound, too. We often don't want to do this; we'd rather just not feel any pain, and if we turn to our addictions, they'll turn off the pain almost instantly. Maybe they won't turn off the pain completely, but they'll turn it off enough that we don't have to feel it, at least for now. Addictions are anything that turn off our emotions now.

There are an infinite number of addictions. We all know the big ones like drugs and alcohol, but there are many more. Others include working too much, being constantly busy, and striving for success. For example, Albert Einstein once said that when anyone he cared about died, he got very busy with his work in order not to have to deal with the pain. There are also more subtle forms of addiction. Some people I know put all their energy into raising their children so they don't have to deal with their unhappy marriages. Others deal with a problem by avoiding it and moving on to something else. They leave the friendship, the job, whatever the problem is, hoping that going on to something else and not dealing with the problem or pain at hand will make it go away and that all will be well.

Addictions can be very subtle. Many people turn to sleeping pills because they can't sleep. Perhaps they can't fall asleep because they are on such a hectic, tight schedule that they need something to calm their racing mind at night. That little pill to help them sleep, instead of being something they need tonight, slowly becomes something they need every night, and it quickly begins to dominate and control their life. It becomes an addiction.

Turning off our feelings doesn't work. Masking them with addictions doesn't solve our problems; they remain . . . unresolved. It's important that we face our feelings and the problems behind them. Just as we wouldn't ignore a serious cut, it's important for us not to ignore serious emotional wounds. Even subtle ones matter.

There's a friend of mine who, every time she has a serious problem with her boyfriend or intimate partner, just leaves him. She doesn't deal with the issue, she doesn't work it out, and she doesn't process it; she just ignores things and moves on to the next relationship. This approach isn't healthy for her because she's building up all these emotional wounds instead of facing them. It's important for us to feel our feelings. It's not hard to do; we just need to face them.

Addictions are very tricky. There are so many of them, and they come in so many disguises that we may not recognize. That's why it's important, in order to avoid addictions, that we do a lot of soul searching. We have to look into our hearts and ask, "How am I doing?" I think the best way to do this is to slow down, look at our lives, and ask further, "Hey, am I using anything on a regular basis that I can't walk away from, that's very important to me, and that I think in a sense I need?" Another way to look at it is to ask, "Am I not wanting to look at something inside me that requires some attention? Is there something I need to focus on and make sure that I'm not turning my feelings off and running away from it?"

The addiction can be subtle. That's why meditation and meditation retreats are very important for our minds and health. They help us look at ourselves so we can know how we are doing. We must remember that we are not smarter than addictions. We must be aware of how things are going in our lives. If we're turning towards something that we can't seem to walk away from, and we know that it's causing us or others to suffer, then we must look at it and say, "Hmmm, what's causing this?" Don't judge it; just look at it and spend some time exploring it. If it's a feeling that needs to be healed, then heal it. If it's a habit, walk away from it. That's the best way to treat addictions.

Let's say we're struggling with a food addiction—we love eating chocolate and often eat too much of it. Each time we feel like eating chocolate, we can instead distract our minds by going for a walk or doing something besides indulging. Walking is one of my favorite ways of turning my mind away from something that is unhealthy for me towards something that is healthy. Going for a walk is an awesome way to focus the mind on something else. Try it; you just might like it!

Addictions are a lot like mosquito bites. That initial desire to scratch the itchy, red bump is very strong, but if we focus our minds on something else, the desire to scratch goes away. So too with addictions, when we feel the pull, if we do something else to take our minds off it, it goes away. Remember, our minds can focus on only one thing at a time. Addictions are fed by thoughts, by creating stories like, "Oh, it would be so great to have that right now." However, if we focus our minds on something else, the desires slowly get weaker and go away. They may keep trying to come back, but if we continue to refocus our minds, they will go away.

There are so many addictions. It may overwhelm us to realize how many things we are addicted to, and that's why I truly encourage everyone who wants to be happy to allow some quiet time. We have to have the peace and tranquility of our meditations to know ourselves. That is truly half the battle of conquering our addictions, our goal towards long-lasting happiness. We can do it; it just takes time, effort, and awareness.

Let's tune into our inner being, taking time to see where we are and what we are feeling, so we can stop numbing ourselves with addictions and live full, happy lives.

Chapter Twelve
Turn Bad Habits into Good Habits

Some of the habits we have are good; some aren't so good. How do we transform our unhealthy habits into good ones?

I'll use myself as an example. I love fudge, and on a trip to Gethsemani in Kentucky, I found the monks there make the most magnificent fudge. Every day, they have a sample for all the retreats. So, before I came home, I ordered myself a box, and since I've been home, I've ordered more because they ship all over the world. Every day, I came home after work and ate a box of fudge. That was a bad habit. Bad habits ultimately lead us towards unhappiness because anything we do that is unhealthy for us is going to cause us suffering. Actually, bad habits can often be seen as addictions. They start with something small but in time become addictive. Addictions leave no room for true, lasting happiness.

The first part of changing habits is to be aware of what we're doing. So many of us have bad habits we're not even aware of. We want to look and say, "Okay, is there something I have been doing that is causing me pain or suffering?" We have to be open to see them and then acknowledge them honestly. Eating a piece of fudge every day may not be that bad, but a whole boxful every day will be. So look at your habits and first acknowledge what you are doing.

Awareness is key because without it we can't change the habit. That's why I recommend every day taking some time for self-reflection and asking yourself, "How is my life going?" Is it doing well? Are you doing things that are healthy for you? An example is exercise. It is healthy for us, and if we're not doing it, what are we doing instead? If we can acknowledge that every day we come home and we spend a couple of hours watching TV to unwind or having a few glasses of alcohol, we have to spot it and say, "Hmm, perhaps this is a bad habit that I need to begin to change." It's important that we are honest because we can really fool ourselves. Think about heroin addicts—doing their drug every day and not even aware of how it is ruining their lives. On some level, of course, they are, but they are in pretty strong denial. So, we need to look at ourselves honestly and ask, "How is this affecting my life now? What is this going to do to me in five, ten, twenty years? How is it going to affect others in my life?"

Habits that we feed get stronger with time. Let's be honest about what we are doing because if we're not aware, we can't change the bad habits into good ones.

The second thing we need to do is create change through kindness and patience with ourselves. Once we discover we have a bad habit, we tend to be very self-critical. But this creates a self-fulfilling prophecy. If we tell ourselves we're bad, bad, bad for doing a bad habit, we're going to stay stuck doing the bad—and stuck for decades. It's actually the negative criticism that causes the bad habit to remain. We live down to that belief that we're bad. When we're critical, we focus on what's wrong. There's a very important question we can ask that will help us, especially because habits take a long time to change: "What can I learn from this?"

Instead of being so highly self-critical, we can see what we can learn from it. Kindness is going to help us more than beating ourselves up. When people get into a drug or alcohol habit, they wake up in the morning after using and are very self-critical. They feel like a terrible person, and even their loved ones might reinforce the behavior. A more positive habit is to go to an AA or NA meeting. So, instead of hearing "I'm bad, I'm bad, I'm bad" all day long, at the meeting, one can learn to separate the self from the action or addiction, build a little self-confidence, and begin to change. Feeling better about oneself and one's ability to change leaves room for getting out of the addiction.

It's the same with any habit. If we are self-critical, we're going to repeat that habit over and over. If we want to blame something or someone for our habits, we could turn to genetics or our conditioning. But criticism of self or others isn't going to do anyone any good. If you make a bad choice, ask what you can learn from it. It might take a bit of time, but we can change that habit.

Since we're using awareness to understand our habits, we're probably going to discover that most of our habits are methods to feel good after a stressful day. For example, when we're tired, when we're exhausted, when we want to come home and need to relax, we might eat fudge, drink a glass of wine, or smoke a joint. We think it will help us deal with stress and relax, but it's bad for us because we can become addicted to the habit. But we remain in awareness here; we don't criticize ourselves but only see what we are doing and why. To change the bad habit, we have to understand that change is going to come from kindness.

So what do we do next? We change habits by actually addressing that stress and doing something differently. It's normal after a long day to be exhausted, and stress happens to a lot of people. Instead of having the fudge or wine at the end of the day, we come up with a good alternative. We ask, "How can I address this stress differently?" We change the habits. Let's say instead of coming right home, we stop at the gym first as a way to eradicate some of that stress. Or, we go to friends and chat about what's going on. Or, we go for a walk in the park. We don't just remove the bad habit; we replace it with a new one.

Now, because the other habit is pretty strong, we may forget a few times, and if we do we can go back to asking, "What can I learn from this?" You might need to set an alarm to remind yourself to go to the gym or meet your friends, for instance. There are many things we can do instead of relying on the old habit.

We might think we just need to be strong and stop the habit, but power of mind is sometimes not enough. If willpower were enough, then everyone who is struggling with an alcohol or drug addiction would easily quit. It doesn't work. What does work is finding a new habit that we can follow. We may need to try several before getting a good one that we stay with. The alcoholic says, "I am going to go to meetings." The person who struggles with a fudge addiction says, "I am going to go for a walk before coming home." All we have to do is begin to see things differently and not resort to attacking ourselves. There are many things we can do differently and we just need to experiment until we find the one that is right for us.

As much as bad habits are created, so are good habits. I love doing yoga. I love walking. And I love meditating. They're very strong habits inside me. I probably will do them until the day I die.

We can all develop good habits. and once in place, they can be difficult to break. So let's change the bad habit into something that we want, but let's do it kindly. Be patient. Each time we do mess up, we can see what we can learn from it. If what we are doing isn't working, then we can try something else that will work and be better for us.

We work on things and can too easily get frustrated and then give up. We hear that self-criticism, and it can be harsh. But if we repeatedly use kindness, it works. We also have to be patient. In time, the good habits will become stronger. So if we work towards changing bad habits, we will be happier.

Let's recap.

First, we have to be aware of what we are doing. We watch our thoughts to see what's going on in our heads all day long.

Second, we need to be kind to ourselves as we work to change. Remember, we can be our harshest critics. We must realize habits come with conditioning, and we need to be kind towards changing that conditioning. When we mess up, we can say, "What can I learn from this?" Kindness works so we have to be kind no matter how long it takes.

Third, we have to change our habits. If we keep doing the same thing and expect different results, we're going to be sorely disappointed. We have to change our habits by trying to do different things until we find something that works. Once we do that over and over, that will become the new habit. But it will be good for us.

Fourth, we need patience. If we have had a habit for ten years, it might take a few years to change it.

We need a positive coach to help us, and the coach we have all day long is the one in our minds. So be kind to yourself and think kind thoughts instead of resorting to damaging self-criticism.

Chapter Thirteen
Three Things to Do
When Bad Things Happen

When we start feeling happier, we might get the idea that we are shielded from any more bad things. Unfortunately, bad things can still happen. Tragedies strike, no matter how great a place we reach in our lives.

This is true even of the most enlightened ones. Buddha lived many years after he had his first enlightenment. Although he lived into his eighties, he didn't remain healthy and fit his whole life; everything didn't only go well for him. People that he loved died, as he got older his body wore out, and he succumbed to illnesses.

Just because we get to that point of happiness, everything is not necessarily going to go smoothly for the rest of our lives. Think of Jesus. His life was cut short. Many people despised him, and in the end, he was very much alone and died a horrible death. A more recent example would be the Dalai Lama. He seems like a very happy and peaceful human being. But he has gone through difficult times. Many of the people he loved have been killed or tortured.

So, it isn't as if everything is going to run easily once we reach a point of living a happy life. That isn't how it works. How can we deal with disaster or heartbreak that enters our lives? That is what matters most. Even when tragedy strikes, we want to deal with it so our lives still proceed beautifully,.

If we live long enough, we will encounter tragedy of some sort. We may lose loved ones, most likely our parents. We may suffer accidents. Some people die quickly but most of us are going to get illnesses and die over an extended period. Very few of us are going to have thirty to forty years of a steady job, after which we retire with the financial means to live well for the rest of our lives. Most of us have ups and downs along the way; we get things, we lose things, things go well, and things don't go so well. This is life.

So how do we deal with tragedy so we can maintain our happiness? Three steps will help. First, we recognize misfortune is part of life. Second, we do what we can to improve the situation.

And three, knowing we've done what we can, we carry on. That all might seem easier to say than do, so let's look at these three in more detail.

First, we have to accept that, no matter what we're given, no matter how well things are going, sooner or later tragedy will hit. Thinking that we can reach a place where we avoid tragedy is a mistake. It is going to happen. That's the main thing: accepting that life is sometimes not going the way we want it to.

Acknowledging that misfortune is going to happen is important. Saying it's unfair or shouldn't be happening is just going to make us suffer needlessly. When we live, we do suffer; it's part of life. Accept this.

It's not necessarily that we're doing something wrong. Life includes things that can't always be prevented; others can make unwise decisions that affect us. But there might be things we need to learn and change. We all make mistakes, and they usually have consequences that hurt.

For example, when people drink and drive, they are usually not trying to hurt someone else. But sometimes they do—their drinking causes them to lose control of their car, get into an accident, and hurt someone. Yes, they made a mistake, but it isn't going to do them any good to say, 'This shouldn't have happened." And if their accident involves another person who was, unfortunately in the wrong place at the wrong time, that person also won't be helped by saying, "This shouldn't have happened."

But it did. "Shouldn't have" deals with the past. It's done, over, can't be changed. Our happiness depends upon now, the present. We need to recognize bad sometimes happens so we can move to the next step. After we've acknowledged we're not exempt from tragedy, we can stop fighting it. It *is* happening, and so we need to work with it.

Second, we see what we can do to make the situation better. What do we have in our power to rectify it right now?

For example, if we got into a car wreck with a drunk driver and it wasn't our fault and now we're in the hospital, we need to get well and become physically fit. So, we go to physical therapy, do the exercises, go to our doctor's appointments, do our treatment, and focus on getting our bodies better. If we need to go to court for the situation, we will. We won't be focusing on what went wrong; that's in the past and will only keep us stuck. Instead, we concentrate on making the present better by healing ourselves.

Let's flip the scenario. If we were the one driving while drunk who caused injury to another, then we must recognize our part, see how we can prevent that happening again, and take appropriate action. We look at our behavior and see what caused us to drink and drive. The number one way to preclude us from being stuck and repeating the same behavior is not beating ourselves up. Part of learning from the situation might be getting involved with therapy or maybe meditating. It's going to be proactively doing things to change our behavior so we don't do it again. We may have to make financial reparations for the damage we've done; we may have to apologize to the people that we've hurt and their families. But we don't beat ourselves up. We just do what we must to make things better as much as we can. We have to differentiate between what we can fix and what we can't. Then we let go of what we can't.

In either case, after we do what needs to be done to get healthy again, then we enjoy life as much as possible. In the hospital, we could talk with the people that are visiting us, read good books, watch movies that make us laugh. Later, we also get outdoors in nature if we can. Mostly what we're spending our time doing is just living life and not even thinking about the tragedy. Even if we're in a wheelchair, no matter how bad that tragedy is, we can do things to make it better.

Think of relationships. Almost everyone is going to go through a breakup or divorce. When someone we love wants to end our relationship, what do we do? We see if we can do something to repair the relationship. We might ask if our partner wants to go to counselling; if we both can talk about it and the other tells us what we did wrong, we can work towards rectifying our behavior. Mostly what we do is focus on what we did wrong so we can do better. It's not to beat ourselves up but. We want to learn from our mistake so that next time, if the other takes us back or if we get into a new relationship, the behavior that was dysfunctional from our part changes for the better. We change it by learning from our missteps.

For instance, if the mistake is that we picked the wrong person, we try to be more scientific about whom we choose and not just let our emotions rule. We change our behavior and thinking and choices that don't serve us well. If they aren't healthy, we see if there is something we can do differently in picking a new partner so we will have a successful relationship.

Let's use the example of illness. Let's say we go to the doctor and we are told we have cancer. So what we proactively do in this situation is research it on the Internet and speak to our doctors. We look at what we can do right now to make our bodies heal. Then we do that, after which we need to move to the next step. This step is about living well now. After we have worked to do everything within our power to fix it, we then have to live life, and we mostly give that tragedy little or no energy.

Three, we move on. We have recognized that invariably tragedy enters life, and we have done what we can. Now, we carry on with life.

Regardless of the tragedy, our dealing with it often involves grieving. As a clinical psychologist, I have found that grieving for about 5 percent of the day is all we need to get well. If, instead for example, people grieve all day long, they tend to be depressed and are not getting better. Grieving is essential towards healing, but it is not something we do continuously; it's a small part of our day, an important part. We can spend a bit of time grieving—or even feeling angry—but mostly we just live.

After a tragedy, our minds will want to go over the accident, breakup, illness, or whatever over and over. Each time we think about it, we can say, "Hmm. Can I do anything about this right now?" If the answer is no, then we don't need to think about it. We drop the thought right then and get back to living. If we're going for a walk, we just walk; if we're with our friends, we're just with our friends. We don't sit around bemoaning the loss. That only keeps us stuck. What we need to do instead is get out there and be active, heal, and distract ourselves. There is time for healing, but there is mostly time for living.

People do tend to spend a lot of time after tragedy just grieving and, thus, staying stuck and not getting better. To get out of this rut, we ultimately distract ourselves with something else. This isn't about distraction in an addictive sense, though. An addictive distraction would be: "I feel bad. I don't want to feel like this, so I'm going to take this." Whatever "this" is—alcohol, drugs, another relationship, food, etc.—it is not the distraction I am talking about. Those are not healthy and not healing.

A positive distraction means living in the moment and not covering up pain with some form of addiction. We get back to living how we have always lived well—by having a childlike approach, enjoying each moment, being present with not thinking about what isn't anymore and what we've lost, not being in the future, not being in the past, but living in the now, enjoying life presently without thoughts, just flowing with life. And again when thoughts about the tragedy sneak in, we ask is there anything we can do right now? If the answer is no, then we get back to just flowing in the now, without all those damaging thoughts of ours. Thoughts are based upon criticism, thoughts are based upon wishing things were different or our desires. When we are in our thoughts, we're not living in the now.

Let's go further with our example of driving drunk and causing a car accident and say we caused someone to die. Now, we have been sent to prison for five years. That's a big deal. What do we do? If we have made amends and have gone to meetings to learn from our mistake, then we approach our prison term this way. We say, "I have five years here. How do I make this work well for me?" With all that time, we have several options—get into good physical shape take some courses that are offered in prison, perhaps learn an online skill, get involved with some groups, even meet some great people. We decide to do things to live well now. Even in prison, we can do that. It's about living in the present moment, wherever we are.

I actually know of a person who is in prison for life, on death row because of some bad choices he made, and he uses that time to develop his meditation practice. He has reached a point where he is very much living in the present moment and living well. We can do that, no matter what hits us, and turn it into something beautiful. There's always something beautiful we can create, no matter how much tragedy strikes.

This can be hard to understand, accept, and do, especially in devastating situations. We might never make sense of them until we go to heaven and God explains all to us. But until we get that answer, mostly we're left with just living in the now and not thinking about the tragedy, unless we can proactively do something about it. No matter how hard things are right now, getting back to the now is always the solution. Living well in the present moment and loving what is, accepting what is, is always the key to happiness.

So in review, there are three things we can do to deal well when things go bad.

1. We acknowledge tragedy is part of life.
2. We do everything in our power to make the situation better.
3. We live life well now, focusing on the beautiful things in our life.

There is always something beautiful to be with—always. So we can have beautiful lives even when bad things happen. Happiness is always there, always available if we choose it.

Chapter Fourteen
Why We Do Bad Things and
How to Change Them

I have been professionally helping people to improve their lives and to achieve happiness for over twenty-five years. There are many ways that I reach out to people—I counsel people in private practice, I give workshops and retreats, I work with corporations, I write books, I post podcasts on my blog, I work with the media. Among the thousands of people that I have come into contact with over the years, I have seen a common theme that keeps them from being happy. It's not lack of resources or lack of love or lack of success. What keeps people from being happy right now is simply self-judgment and the judgment of others.

In other words, we are hard on ourselves and, to a lesser extent, on those around us. When we mess up, we have an incredible tendency to berate ourselves, to speak horribly about ourselves, and to beat ourselves up. It can be awful! The more we hate ourselves, the less we share with other people. We put up walls, making sure others don't get in because we don't want other people to hurt us more than we're already hurting ourselves. It already hurts too much!

Some people who have done a lot of damage and who have caused a lot of havoc in life truly despise themselves. Over the years, I have had the opportunity of talking with people who have committed what our culture considers heinous crimes. Often, we think these people get away with their misdeeds without caring, but actually, the exact opposite is often true. Very often, these people truly hate themselves, and it is very sad.

When we mess up, who is the one to blame? Mind you, our mess-ups may not be so big, but they still matter to us and affect the manner in which we treat ourselves and others. If we behave harshly towards ourselves and one another, we are not going to be happy. So, who is at fault when we mess up or when others mess up? Who is to blame? And similarly, when we succeed and accomplish wonderful things in life, who is the one who should get credit? Who is the one who can say, "Yay, I did it!"? Who is the one who gets credit for succeeding in life? Failure and success are all about volition. Who is responsible? When I succeed, did I do it? When I fail, did I do it?

Responsibility can be broken down into two parts. The first part is genetics, our DNA. We don't choose our DNA; it's given to us at birth. If we are born with blond hair and blue eyes, although we may disguise these traits cosmetically, we will always have them. How greatly genetic influence is involved in who we are is debatable. Most scientists agree it's somewhere between 25 and 50 percent, with some factors as low as 10 percent or some, such as gender, as high as 100 percent. However, whether we like chocolate or love Shakespearean plays is influenced more by our conditioning than genes. Conditioning is the second half of responsibility.

Let's explore conditioning. We don't choose our parents, and we don't choose the environment in which we are raised. As we get older, we start making what seem to be our own choices, but these choices are immensely influenced by the environment and our experiences in our earlier years.

For example, if you ask doctors why they chose that profession, many will mention how, while growing up, they knew someone who was ill whom they cared for, and this is what inspired them. Of course, they needed to have the predisposition to do well in school. But their career choice was mostly based on their environment, including perhaps also, their parents pushing them to succeed in life.

I say we make choices, but academics have debated how much free will we have. To be honest, scholars have pretty much settled upon the idea that there really isn't any. We are what and who we are because of our conditioning; we have no choice or free will. We are conditioned beings. There's still debate out there, of course, but brilliant scientists and philosophers around the world mostly agree that we are products of our environment.

When looking at doing something wrong and wondering who gets the blame, let's suspend talk of the mentally ill and psychopaths, studying instead regular people like you and me who do care when we mess up and hurt people. Why do we do things that we supposedly don't want to do? Who is at fault? It is mainly our conditioning's fault, along with a small contribution from our genetics. This is why we can say, "Yup, I'm forty pounds overweight, and everyone in my family is forty pounds overweight." We are very much products of our environment. Our conditioning shapes us.

In some cultures, people are a lot more relaxed about achievement. These people would sooner sit and enjoy being with family and friends than put time into making a success of a business or their career. There's absolutely nothing wrong with this. However, because of this tendency, these people are less likely to be successful financially. This is a product of their environment.

Let's take a look at when we mess up, when we do something wrong. Why do we do it? In every instance, we can go back and figure out why we do things based on our conditioning. This process may seem cumbersome, but you can begin by asking, "What in my conditioning caused me to do this?" For instance, if I cheated on my wife, did my father cheat on my mother? Did I come from a culture where it was acceptable for a man to cheat on his wife? If that's so, it may be harder for you to be faithful to your spouse. The conditioning we experience early in life shapes us in profound ways.

In the same way, when we succeed in life, it's because of our conditioning. If we felt a lot of pressure, especially from our parents, to succeed in life, then most likely, we did make high achievements. The conditioning we're being exposed to throughout our lives is going to shape us. There's no way to get around this.

So here's the good news: when we fail in life, it's really not our fault. It's the conditioning's fault. Conversely, when we succeed, it's also due to the conditioning. It's a conditioned success.

We don't have to worry about what people think about us. We don't have to worry about anything! What we have to do is simply change the conditioning. If we're conditioned to eat healthy foods, then of course we're not going to want to change that. But, if we eat poorly, then we're going to want to change. If we grew up in an environment where men cheated, then we're going to have to realize that infidelity isn't an acceptable act and isn't good for a successful relationship. We have to start socializing with others who don't believe in cheating and who consider fidelity very important and healthy in having a relationship.

Changing our lives is pretty basic: it's simply a matter of changing the conditioning. It takes work, but it is entirely possible. We will soften and be less ruled by pride and jealousy because we will realize that our environment shapes us. Our environment causes us to be who we are.

If we truly understand that it's the conditioning's fault for the way we are, then we won't be hard on ourselves. We will get softer, kinder towards ourselves, and make room for happiness to appear.

When we beat ourselves up, we continue to do the same things that we hate doing. It's a self-fulfilling prophecy. If I say, "I'm fat," then guess what? I'm going to be fat. If instead I say, "My conditioning caused this. I need to change my conditioning," then I'm going to eat better and get healthier foods.

If we want to place the blame, let's give it to our conditioning. Remember that we can change our conditioning and change ourselves for the better.

Chapter Fifteen
Change Our Beliefs, Stop Our Suffering

When I go to work every day, I drive through the beautiful town of Laguna Beach. It's an artistic community right along the water, and it truly is a lovely place to visit.

When I stopped there once with my dog, Einstein, it was a beautiful day, and there were many other people outside enjoying the lovely weather. As I was walking, a man coming towards was on a collision course if both of us didn't change our directions. So I started moving to the right, and he started moving to the left. Though we weren't going to collide, we were still quite close to each other. Right when we passed each other, he took his shoulder and slammed it pretty hard into mine. My first emotional reaction was one of shock and a little bit of anger because I thought to myself, "Wow! Why did he do that?" I had politely smiled at him, as I often do when I pass someone, and I was working hard at getting out of his way so I knew I hadn't done anything wrong. As far as I knew, I hadn't done anything that had directly upset him. So I turned around and said, "Are you okay? I'm sorry. I didn't mean to bump into you." He just nodded, but you could tell he knew that I knew what had happened. It ended then and there; nothing escalated from it, and I just went on my way.

When I thought about it afterwards, I know what most people would have done in that situation. They would have yelled at him and confronted him, saying things like, "Hey, what's wrong with you? Why'd you do that? What's wrong?" or "Come on, knock it off!" When we do this, we're letting that person's bad day become our bad day. We're giving them the power to control us and affect us. But quite often, when something negative starts, it has very little to do with us. Usually it's a mistake or a misunderstanding, but then we transform that misunderstanding or miscommunication into something ugly or painful.

The fact is we don't have to do that! If we're choosing to live a happy life, we can, instead, respond in a way that doesn't escalate, doesn't lead to more distress, and does diffuse the situation.

Unfortunately most people choose to react. We learn this from a very young age. For instance, listen to parents when their children hurt themselves. For example, little Sarah bumps herself on a chair, and the father might say, "Bad chair! Bad, bad chair! Why'd you hurt Sarah?" He has Sarah get mad at the chair, and then Sarah gets over it and goes on and plays. Because we do this at such a young age, we make this behavior a natural part of our life, and when someone hurts us, we assume we must return in kind. That way of thinking is why we have wars that go on all over the world so often and for so long. When we return hurt with hurt, the pain just keeps going on and on and on.

But truly, all of the suffering that goes on comes from within us. It comes from our false belief that we need to be upset when someone does something hurtful to us. It's like that man who bumped me that day; he could have ruined my day, and then many peoples' days would have been ruined as I continued passing on the hurt.

But that's not my belief. My belief is that I try to be kind towards people. Sometimes I make mistakes, and I apologize when I do, but mostly I work hard at being kind towards people. When someone isn't very kind back towards me, it usually has little or nothing to do with me, and I realize that so I don't get upset. When I drive, I don't get upset when people cut me off because I realize that they're probably just having a really bad day. Because I care for people, I don't want to add to their bad day. I want people to have a good life, so why would I want to make someone who's already miserable even more miserable by getting mad at them?

Self-interest comes into play here, also. Do I want to let other people make my day a bad day, or would I rather have a good life, a happy life and not let others affect me negatively? If I change the way I think about things, then the whole reality changes, even if somebody is yelling at me because I did something to him. I don't have to go to the place where I fight back. I have many options: I can say something genuinely nice to him, I can walk away, I can call him on it, and so on. But I don't have to let others ruin my day. If they ruin my day, then I let them do so.

Perhaps a better way of seeing it is that if I let someone ruin my day because my belief system says that I have rights and I'm going to be angry if I'm not given those rights to various things throughout life, then I'm going to be upset for the rest of my life. The belief system is what's causing that unhappiness. Many people, no matter what example of wrong has been done to them, have come out of painful events well and are happy in their lives. Yes, we have to go through the healing process and set up boundaries, of course; but most of our suffering comes from our false beliefs.

Let's say we go to our doctor and she tells us we have cancer and we probably have two years to live. We have choices now, and our beliefs will affect us. Maybe we believe, "Oh my goodness, this is going to be horrible, and I'm going to have to go through chemotherapy and radiation. I'm going to lose my hair, and I'm going to be in pain. Why is this happening to me?" Then we will be miserable and suffer for the next two years.

But instead, we might say—and there are many people out there that have said this—"Hey, I now only have a couple years of my life left to live. I know there's going to be suffering, but I'm going to do everything in my power to live a simply beautiful life and live to the fullest every day." Guess what? That's what's going to happen to our life as we move through what could be a miserable time.

Our beliefs shape our reality. So if we want to have a happy life, we have to know what we believe. If we believe that the world is a dark, miserable, cruel place, then that's what we will experience. But if we believe that most of the suffering and pain experienced in life comes from misunderstanding, miscommunication, and other sources and it's really not about "me," then we simply flow with life and our lives go well.

Yes, as we go through life, sometimes people are going to bump into us and hit us in the shoulder, sometimes pretty hard. But after we feel that initial reaction, then our beliefs shape how the encounter ends and how it keeps going. Will we respond in kind and let that other person's misery become ours, or will we realize that this probably has nothing to do with us personally and let it go? We can have a beautiful life, no matter what's happening in our world. What we need to work towards is accepting what is and loving what is, and then we will have a beautiful life.

The change we need in order to have this beautiful life is within us. Yes, we'll do some changing externally, but ultimately, the change we need to make is within our own hearts. When we change, the whole universe changes.

Chapter Sixteen
The Root Cause of Our Suffering and How to End It

Do we ever wonder how it all started? How did we ever get to that point where we're filled with so much anxiety and stress in life? When did it all begin? Where does this anxiety, this worry, this suffering come from, and how do we change it?

To answer, we have to go back in history to the dawn of humankind. Let's look at what the environment was like for those early humans. What did they have to face? It's important to know this because we've evolved from them and they have passed on their evolutionary process, a genetic predisposition, which affects us and causes us to suffer.

Thousands of years ago, we didn't have buildings, armies, and police officers that protected us. We lived out in the wild. Every time we went outside, there was the potential of finding food, but there was also the risk of becoming food. We woke up in the morning hungry, so we searched for food, knowing that we had to be careful not to become food. The best way we did that was by being very circumspect; behind every bush, every hill, every place we searched, we were on the lookout for any possible danger. The people who were mellow, relaxed, and peaceful probably didn't survive. What Charles Darwin discovered over a century ago was that those who survived were the fittest. You could survive if you were highly alert, cautious, and anxious about what was behind the bush that might eat you.

Nowadays, if you think about places where wild animals reside, you can see how smaller animals, such as rabbits, are at risk. If those creatures are relaxed, laid-back, just kicking it, and eating grass without being aware of their surroundings, they are going to become a predator's meal. The ones that we often see are very fast and cautious, and they look afraid. They are protecting their lives. It was the same in the beginning of our humanoid time. Those that survived were the most neurotically nervous because they survived, even though they didn't have the best quality of life. It is this survival instinct that has been passed on.

Our environment has changed tremendously since then. We don't need to be so nervous because we have buildings to protect ourselves, hired people to guard our territories, and police officers and armies to protect us. However, it's unfortunate that instead of letting go of our nervous habits, we tend to hang onto them.

But what predators today are we are so afraid of? They are many, but they all boil down to two things: fear and desire.

We become fearful of things we could lose and of bad things happening to us. Even if we're well and everything's going great, we can be fearful of losing things that are important to us. That's half of it.

The other half is desire. We think if we have a big-enough home, a big-enough bank account, we're going to be safe, and everything will be great. We bounce between these two emotions, fears and desires. We want to protect ourselves and find a safe home, perhaps have the most successful job in the world so that everyone will look up to us. But then anxieties arrive. The same anxiety of predators now gets placed onto these mental fears and desires that are certainly not life-threatening and really sort of silly, especially if you consider how many people around the world have nothing.

Living in the United States, most of us have enough food for at least a week, if not years. And we have shelter. Most likely, we don't have anything to worry about that would affect our survival. For the most part, we probably don't have fears over basic human needs, and yet we are so fearful. We have so much more than many people around the world, and yet our desires are inexhaustible. We never have enough. If we think about it, we probably know that.

When we were younger, maybe we wanted a car, a girlfriend or boyfriend, to finish high school, and to do something with our lives. We thought that if we achieved that, our lives would be blessed. Shortly afterwards, it was good for a while, but then new desires and fears kicked in. Again, it's the idea that the lion is going to get us or not leave us alone. For cave people, that mentality made sense because there were wild animals all around. Now we are so far removed from that way of living, and yet we experience the same anxieties those cave people did.

The truth is that we can be happy right now as long as we're willing to realize that we mostly live in a paradise. Everything that we have we don't need much of to be happy. We have food, we have a safe place to live, and more. We can be very happy, but our minds cause us to be unhappy. That's where it all stems from. Thousands of years ago, what was the survival tool now has become a neurotic obsession, and so we still struggle.

Enough of that! We are now going to come up with a plan that overcomes our neuroses and live life well. There are two things we can do to deal with the neuroses—be aware and be with what is.

First comes awareness and assessing the danger. When we are nervous, fearful, and spending a lot of time and energy thinking about something, we begin to observe our thoughts. We start paying attention to what we are thinking about right now. We can say, "Oh, I realize I'm nervous right now. I'm worried something's going to happen." Once we look at what's going on in our minds, we can realize what is plaguing us. It could be a variety of things. It could be worries over scoring an A in a course or not having enough money to pay the bills three months from now. Since our minds are experts at creating stories, we have to ask ourselves, "Is this a lion type of crisis right now? Is the lion going to eat me? Or do I need to find shelter, create a home so that I'm safe? Is it about the desire to have a safe home, or is it a fear that I'm going to be eaten right now?" If the fear doesn't match the magnitude of a lion eating us, then we can do something instead of worrying. We can start to make changes.

We don't need much to be happy. Some of the happiest people I've met have live in monasteries. They inhabit the same territory as other people, and they have nothing, yet they are happy. I have met people in hospitals dying of cancer, and they've been very happy, even with the pain, so we don't need much to be happy, to be content right now. So, we can ask ourselves, "How important is this thought?" Then, we ask if you we can do something about it. If we need a new job, we can go online and search for one. Great, then we can put our worrying energy towards other things. The fear is of a lion we can move away from.

Now comes the the second part, living with what is. What if there is nothing we can do about the fears? We have to see that what is happening right now is something that we can *be* with. What is going on right now that we're not paying attention to? Perhaps we're sitting down for a meal and it's a good meal, but we're rushing through it. Take the time to slow down and be in the moment. Perhaps we're with someone else but we're not listening to what the person is saying. We can slow down our thoughts and tune in to their words and be present with them. We miss so much about our lives because we're not there; we're in our heads, we're fearful, we're nervous, we're neurotic. So this is all about being present and loving what is. There's always something beautiful we can be with in our lives.

We can take the time to see and appreciate what is around us—looking at the sky above, having a meaningful conversation with friends, listening to the wind blowing in the trees, savoring our meals. There are so many things we can do to have beautiful lives, especially since our lives just aren't that dangerous anymore. We live in a pretty safe world. I know there are exceptions to this, of course, but unfortunately what we're often doing is living neurotic lives because we're letting that part of our mind that's there to protect us make our lives miserable instead. We are see lions that are not even there. For a happy life, we have to stop seeing everything as a crisis.

Let me use an example that illustrates this. A few Christmases ago, I was at a family gathering with many of my relatives. One of my nieces who is in high school was on her phone texting people throughout the time we were together. It was amazing how little conversation we could have because she was often looking at her phone and checking messages. At one point, I decided to do an experiment. I picked her phone up from where she had set it down and put it in my pocket. At first, nothing happened, but then I saw she couldn't find her phone and became frantic. She was very upset, asking, "Where's my phone? Where's my phone?" as if she having withdrawal pains. A few minutes later, I gave her back her phone with my apologies. She got her drug fix again, and then she was fine. We can make almost anything into a lion crisis.

When something appears drastic, we have to ask ourselves, "Is this really something that I need to get upset over, or am I missing out on life?" When we are in crisis mode, we stop noticing things around us. We don't notice the blooming flowers or the fiery sunsets or the tantalizing dinner. Being in that state of constant stress blinds us to the beauty around us.

Things are not going to go well for us all the time. So, after we have determined that we are not in crisis, that a lion isn't going to eat us, then we can do what we can just to be present with what is. We can soak in all the beautiful things around us—even if we are just at our desk working. Whatever we are doing, we can enjoy it. We can be driving home and listening to beautiful music and then get home and go for a walk.

There are so many things we can do to make life beautiful right now. When we get out of our heads and we learn to live in the present moment, life goes well. We can start being less critical and neurotic by understanding where those thoughts come from. We don't have to be so fearful if we learn to trust that everything is going to work out. If we live our lives one day at a time, one hour at a time, they can be beautiful.

So, to recap, we get out of our suffering, first, by observing our thoughts, seeing what we're thinking, and gauging the real danger. Is that lion going to eat us? Second, if there is no crisis, we just be with what is. We can learn to love it. We have been conditioned to fear and worry, so the changes won't happen overnight, but if we work on it every day, we can become better at it and have beautiful lives.

Chapter Seventeen
How Suffering Can Make You Stronger

Suffering, painful events, and bad things happen to us as human beings; this is something we all go through in life. We are going to suffer. It's inevitable and part of the human condition.

But how can we deal with suffering? What are our options? We have three choices available to us:

- We can suppress our feelings.
- We can feel our feeling.
- We can grow from them.

The first option, we can suppress them, is often the most tempting and easiest option and is, therefore, what many people choose to do. It's one reason there is so much suffering in the world because when we suppress our suffering it doesn't go away; it just gets put aside for a little bit, and then we need to suppress it more.

Let me use an example to illustrate this. Have you ever seen a film where someone breaks up with the love of his life, goes off and gets drunk for two or three days in a row, comes out of it, and then moves on? No. Never! That's not what happens. The drunken bender doesn't solve a thing. The suffering returns. All the person has done is suppress the pain from the break-up. This is an amazingly common scenario. When we suffer, we often turn to substances or sometimes to other people. In other words, we turn to things outside ourselves to try to turn off the suffering.

I once gave a talk to a group of people about suffering, and a woman came up to me later and said, "You're exactly right, Dr. Puff. My husband died five years ago, and, within a year, I remarried. I didn't want to face the loss of my husband so I remarried thinking it would resolve my suffering, and it hasn't gone well."

There are infinite examples I could give about this way of dealing with suffering because people choose this suppress-the-feelings option all the time. Suffering occurs. Instead of feeling it, we numb it. But that doesn't work for very long, so we have to keep numbing it and turn to more addictions to help us not feel our feelings. And we have so many addictions available to us to avoid feeling—food, prescription medications, relationships, keeping super busy, and so on. We all know what they are because we've all done it. Instead of feeling our feelings, we try to distract ourselves. We turn to these addictions because they work; they do shut off the pain, temporarily. The problem is that, over time, what starts with us eating a box of cookies because we're sad ends up with us being three hundred pounds overweight; now we're really depressed, and so we continue to turn to our addiction for food.

The second option we can take when dealing with suffering is that we can feel our pain. Some call it owning our pain. If we feel our pain, it is challenging to us. Going back to the example of losing a loved one, we do suffer when we feel that loss. It can be very sad, even tragic. Tears can flow, as well as anger from that loss. However, what happens is that feeling or owning the pain helps us get better. Our suffering heals, and then we move on.

The third option occurs when we let the pain pass through us, making room for growth. We can grow from our feelings of suffering. We can learn from our experience, our suffering, and adapt that experience into our lives because the pain is healed. We have then put ourselves in a position to use these experiences of suffering as learning tools for making good choices throughout the rest of our lives.

Now let's take this talk about suffering to a deeper level, about how life is ultimately fair in regards to suffering. Fair? Did I say suffering is fair in life? Yes, I did. That statement may ruffle a few feathers, but hang in there and let me explain what I mean.

What most people do when they experience suffering is choose the first option—they numb it. And the numbing works! It doesn't totally take the pain away, but it does lessen the suffering. It's very unhealthy for us in the long run, only a temporary fix, of course, and keeps us returning to our addictions to continue numbing the pain.

I know a lot of people struggle with kids and suffering. They say, "Well, Dr. Puff, what about little kids? They suffer. They can't take the pain away." I frequently work with little children who have gone through some very horrific things. And most of them take this first route—they numb the pain. When they go through suffering, they actually shut down. It's almost as if God puts a natural painkiller inside them so they are able to withdraw from the pain. The first time they may actually confront and deal with the pain is when they are in therapy with me. Or they suppress it until later in their lives when they're adults, and they finally decide they need to deal with their pain. Mostly what they do is distract themselves from their pain. Many people have told me how they see themselves floating up in a corner watching themselves being abused and not even feeling pain until they get into therapy with me. Most of what they've done in their lives is run away from the pain.

So, of course, it isn't healthy for us to use painkillers or addictions in order to numb our feelings. But we choose the addictions because they work, so that's why we use them.

However, we do have another choice. We can decide to feel the feelings, to own them, to confront them head on, to deal with them, and that's when the real pain kicks in. The good news is that by feeling the pain and the suffering, we get better. So yes, now there is pain, but there's an end to this pain when we deal with it, when we confront it, when we feel our feelings. We heal.

I think recovering alcoholics are excellent examples of this. They are in pain, so they drink, and the alcohol helps them numb their pain. When they decide to stop using alcohol as a painkiller, they have a huge challenge. Without their drinks, suddenly, all that pain comes back. In order to deal with the pain, they go to AA meetings to get support. They work through their pain, and then they can start working on improving their lives. When we go through our pain, we ultimately walk away from it a deeper, richer, fuller, and stronger person. Experiencing suffering and dealing with it successfully helps us grow.

Often there's a direct correlation between the amount of suffering we experience and the amount of growth that we experience. If you ever want to prove this point to yourself, just think of people you feel have done the most with their life. If you know them. ask for their life story. Or, if they are famous person, seek out their biography, and see how much suffering they went through to get to where they are. I think you will find, without exception, that people who are very deep have gone through a great deal of suffering. That's just how life works; we grow through suffering. Yes, it's hard; yes, it's challenging. People who have dealt with suffering and have come out on the other side are not likely to say they wish that they could go through it again, but they all realize their suffering was important in making them who they are right now. Without that suffering, the great depth inside of them wouldn't be there.

This is why I think the Universe, or God, is ultimately fair. God has given us three choices about how to deal with our suffering. We can decide to numb it and not feel it. It does work in the short term, which just causes us to need more numbing, but it does keep working.

God also gives us the choice to feel our feelings. Initially, that's hard to do. But when we do, we ultimately embrace the third choice, which is growing through the process. So in the end, we're a deeper, fuller, stronger, more spiritually grounded being, and that's good. That's the benefit of going through suffering and not suppressing it. In the end, it turns out well.

Chapter Eighteen
How to Respond with Kindness
When Others React with Anger

Do you ever get upset at someone and then afterwards ask yourself why you got so upset? We all have instances in our lives when we wish we didn't reacted in the way we did. So how do we not react negatively to someone who makes us upset?

We have some deeply ingrained behaviors to correct in ourselves because our actions are conditioned from a very young age. I clearly see this happening in my two children as they repeat what I used to do with my sister. One of them does something to the other that is unjustified, and then the other one will react in kind. They often do the exact same thing back to each other. It's almost as if we are born with the mantra of an eye for an eye; we get revenge by hurting the person back. We might have learned this from a very young age, but unfortunately, many people never grow out of such behavior. They live their lives thinking, "I'm gonna get them when they get me."

One of the most important things wrong with this line of thinking is that we often don't know *why* others act as they do. Often there is just a misunderstanding that has occurred. Something makes us upset about how others conducted themselves, but in all likelihood, they didn't mean to hurt us. But when we heard what they said or saw what they did, we immediately thought that we wanted to hurt them back. We might not have looked at any possible reasons for why they did what they did. Rather, we just reacted in kind.

There's a way to test if we are doing this. When you're out and about, let's say you're purchasing something at the store and the clerk is being rather rude from your perspective, go ahead and ask, "Hey, how's your day going?" What you may find, and what I have often found, is that their day isn't going very well. Perhaps the previous customer was being rude to them, perhaps they just broke up with their boyfriend or girlfriend, perhaps their father is sick in the hospital and they are worried about him. There's a platter of reasons why people act unkindly, and if we can accept that, it can be helpful because we'll begin to see that usually when others do something to us, there is some underlying reason that has very little to do with what we did. It's often not personal and has nothing to do with us. Or sometimes, they might have misunderstood our behavior and thought *we* were the ones being rude, so they were rude back to us. I think often when something happens it truly is a misunderstanding, but when we react in kind or we react more intensely it doesn't become a misunderstanding anymore. We start a revenge cycle.

Now you may be thinking, "But I don't want people to abuse me; I don't want people to treat me badly. " I understand that, and boundaries are very important. But discovering why others did what they did can help us with setting a boundary. If we can acknowledge what they did with, "Hey, what you're doing right now maybe isn't that great," we give them an opportunity to change, to do something different. When we react in kind, however, we follow the eye for an eye way of being, which is not positive at all.

I have found that when people react in kind in a negative way, when they get other people back, they are very unhappy. Here are two stories that illustrate the negativity of an eye for an eye. I once met a woman whose life was very hard. She had so many physical problems, along with broken relationships with family and friends, and was one of the most miserable people I have ever met. Then, I understood why. She told me that when someone hurt her she made sure she always got that person back. I thought, "Yeah, you do that, but your life hasn't turned out that well *because of that.*" When we are harsh towards others, we are the ones that suffer; that harshness comes right back to us.

Think about the meanest person that you know and ask yourself if you would want to be that person. Of course, you don't. Mean people are unhappy and have unhappy lives, and we want to have happy lives, so let's not choose the path of being mean.

Here's the other story. When I was in graduate school, I had the opportunity to spend a summer in the Middle East. Back then, like now, there was a lot of trouble going on. I spent time talking with some people over there, and whether they were Jewish, Christian, or Muslim, they all told me the same thing. They were fighting because the enemy had killed their father, killed their uncle, killed their sister . . ., and they were going to get them back. Although we can understand wanting revenge when someone kills a person that we love, taking that route solves nothing. This fighting for revenge has been going on for thousands of years, and no one knows when it will end. How can it when the killing—and feeling for revenge—continue?

This desire for revenge happens on lesser levels but can escalate into the dangerous. For instance, once when I was in graduate school and working in New York City, I was waiting on the toll roads. I was underneath the tunnel getting into the city, and two motorists were vying for the position into the toll road. They started honking and screaming at each other and got out of their cars and had a fist fight about it. Sometimes people get so angry they feel like lashing out.

We feel justified at being upset, but I know there is someone on this planet who'd be in the exact same situation and wouldn't be upset. And this isn't to judge ourselves; it is so we can learn that we don't necessarily have to be upset. We can be at a restaurant where the waiter is rude to everybody, but only one person in the whole restaurant gets upset. Or, we can be driving and see that a rude driver is cutting off a lot of people, but only one person is honking.

Forgiveness, letting go of that anger, is what leads toward a peaceful and beautiful life. Hanging onto our anger is living life in misery forever. It just never goes away if we don't let go of our negative feelings and desire for revenge.

So, how do we do this? When we're with our family or friends and encounter situations where they have done something that upsets us, what can we do? How do we not lash out at them? It's actually very simple. No matter what situation we find ourselves in or how someone has hurt us, we can change our focus from their behavior to why we are upset. What's inside of us that is causing us to be upset? We can say, "Okay, I am feeling upset right now. Why am I upset?"

Not everyone in this situation would be upset by this, and even if most people would be, we can decide that we don't want to be. It's a choice we have. We can make sure that we set healthy boundaries, that what we do in a dysfunctional situation is focus on how we can respond in a loving, kind way. Boundaries can be loving and kind if we don't allow them to hurt us. And if we don't allow people to hurt us, we're actually helping them. By not reacting to their behavior and by, instead, setting boundaries, we're going to create a very good situation.

We don't have to be upset. Most of the time what we think justifies our anger is a misunderstanding or from overreacting because we're exhausted. We can slow down and tell ourselves it's okay: "I know I'm feeling upset right know about what that person just did, but I don't need to react. I just need to get away from the situation. I need to take a breath. I need to pause and say I don't have to be upset here." We can actually stop feeling upset once we start doing this because it changes our responses. It prevents us from suppressing our feelings. When we learn not to react, we allow ourselves to express our feelings in loving ways, acknowledge them, and then find a healthier outlet for them, such as going for a walk, working out at the gym, or calling a friend and telling them what happened. These are better than lashing out at the person who hurt us. We can then focus on what's happening inside us.

The eye-for-an-eye path can be a dark and painful one. Bypassing it and, instead, controlling our responses puts us on a more powerful and happier path. We can say, "What is my response? What am I feeling? How do I work towards changing it? How do I want to make sure that once I take care of myself I don't put myself in negative situations?" It's a shift from what we've done most of our lives—focus on what the other person is doing wrong and react to it—to focusing on what is happening inside ourselves that's causing us to be upset. Then, it's looking at what we can do to change this within ourselves.

We need to look at the thoughts feeding this reaction, this conditioning that cause us to feel upset, angry, or frustrated. If we shift and look at the situation from a different, calmer, perspective, we can see that it might have nothing to do with us; we might see that we made a mistake. There are so many ways we can change things when we focus on what we need to do differently. We also have to see that there's not much we can do to change another's behavior when someone is acting inappropriately. We can avoid being abused by leaving the situation.

If we are in a situation that is very challenging and choose not to react, we can discover options and power that would otherwise be lost when reacting negatively to the other person. Our non-response might also help the others and let them think about their behavior. When we react negatively to them in kind, we give them justification for their behavior. They may then think about what *we* did wrong, while we're thinking about what they did, and the cycle continues. Our not reacting stops that cycle.

Here is an example from my work with couples that are in abusive situations. When one person is being physically or emotionally abusive to the other, usually both play that dance. One acts inappropriately, but the other person participates in it, maybe by provoking the partner. I teach them not to do that dance, not to think about what the other person did wrong. It can be best to think, "I didn't really do anything wrong. They were rude and acted inappropriately, so it might be time for me to leave the situation."

We might wonder how people can stay in such a situation. Often, their participation holds them to it; they are part of the dance and don't think to let go. Obviously, they are not exactly at the same level of the abuser, but they are participating nonetheless. If they stop participating, it's much easier for them to walk away from it instead of engaging with the behavior. Later on, once removed from the abusive relationship, they might think about what they did wrong and become hard on themselves. But by not reacting to the other person in the first place, they have nothing for which to criticize themselves.

No matter what people do to us, the person that is always harshest on us is ourselves because we know what we did. There can be many reasons for why people do things to us, but we know what we did. So if we learn not to react by setting boundaries, looking at ourselves, and asking, "Why is this causing me to be upset? How is my ego getting caught up in this?" then we learn how to diminish our ego and involvement.

When we lessen our ego, we also learn how to diminish our attachments, our fears, our desires, and we live far more in the present. If we live in the present moment, we allow ourselves to observe the situation.

Allow yourself to observe, not to participate or create stories that go along with it. Instead of focusing on others and what they did wrong, you can focus on why you are upset. Look closely at your feelings and ask yourself what you can do or how you can think differently. Ask yourself how you could react in another way so as not to be so upset. Again, this doesn't mean to be a marshmallow and allow people to walk on you—boundaries are often necessary. However, I am encouraging you to focus on why you feel upset and to stop focusing on what others are doing wrong, as well as how you can stop feeling bad even if they continue to do this behavior. "What can I do differently to not be upset in this situation?" is something we can ask ourselves.

Even if we have stories of horrible things that have happened to us, there are many things we can do not to feel upset. As long as one person on the planet wouldn't be upset in this situation, then that means it's a possibility for us. Let's move in that direction of not being upset. Let's not allow other people to ruin our life.

We're here to have beautiful lives, and the way to achieve that is by focusing on ourselves and making sure we are taking the path that's peaceful and happy, living in the present moment right now.

Chapter Nineteen
What Mosquitoes and Anger Have in Common

Why do we get angry, and how do we keep ourselves from being angry so we can live a happy life?

I grew up in Iowa where, every summer, we could expect one thing to happen: mosquitoes. As the summer advanced, so did mosquito population. But we knew what to do. First, we protected ourselves from the mosquitoes with bug spray or with smoke from a fire. Second, if they bit us, the key is not to scratch but leave it alone. If we scratched the bite, it only got worse and itched even longer. Since we knew that every summer the mosquitoes would be coming, we didn't let it upset or anger us. We dealt with the situation because we knew life had mosquitoes in it during Iowa summers.

Although we were prepared, visitors who had never experienced mosquitoes might not have been. They might have reacted differently and gotten angry over the biting bugs, asking, "Why are there mosquitoes? Why are they here?" By focusing on the mosquitoes, they would ruin their days of summers.

We do the same with our anger. We let things that happen in life, like mosquitoes, upset us, get us angry, and sometimes even ruin our lives. Why do we do this? Why do we get angry? Why do we let situations upset us? Invariably, we assume someone else or an event is intentionally doing something to us. This is the same as assuming mosquitoes are trying specifically to bite us and hurt us personally and then reacting by wanting to get them back and allowing them to ruin our days because they were hurting us! We do the same thing with people: we assume that they are doing something to us and so we become angry with them.

Let's use a simple example. We're driving a car, and someone cuts us off and honks at us, driving crazily. We get angry with them. But we don't really know why that person got upset. Maybe he lost his job that day or had a fight with a loved one; maybe he was rushing to the hospital because he was sick; maybe he was extremely stressed. There are many reasons why other people do what they do, and rarely does it have anything do with us.

Instead of thinking this, though, we assume they're wrong and we're in the right and now we have the right to be angry with them. But when we do that, we are giving them power over us. We're letting them, through our thoughts, make us angry and unhappy. We don't have to do that. When a mosquito bites us, we don't get angry with the bug. We know mosquitoes are part of life. Likewise, if we're driving a car and people cut us off, that's just part of driving; that's what happens because sometimes people do things that are inappropriate.

It's like mosquitoes biting us to hurt us. That's silly, isn't it? Rarely do people intentionally try to hurt us; they may do things that hurt do us, but it's not because they are focused on hurting us. It's more like a domino effect: they're upset about something and lashing out at the world, and we get in the way.

Now, when it happens—when we get in their way—we have a choice. Do we keep the dominoes falling, take on their anger, and pass it back to them and on to other people? Or do we say in our mind, "This probably has nothing to do with me so I'm going to let it go and just live my life well"?

Our minds create stories that certain events are wrong or people shouldn't do certain things or, if they do, then we need to get back at them. This is how wars and feuds begin, with hatred continuing for decades and even centuries.

What we need to do is first see that most of the time when people do things to us it's so much like those mosquitoes: we're just in the wrong place at the wrong time, and it has nothing to do with us. If we live long enough, we're going to get bitten by mosquitoes and we're going to have something else—maybe even many somethings—bad happen to us. It's inevitable, but all we can do is not to let our minds create a story about it, not think we have been wronged, and not believe we need to take our revenge. We don't have to participate in that. All we have to do is say, "Oh, that's too bad this happened. I wish it hadn't happened. I want to do things to stop it from happening. I can decide to live right now. I will just walk away from this situation." These are the things we can do to stop the situation from hurting us unnecessarily.

Most important, we must not engage with our minds and judge things as right or wrong. Sometimes we get bitten by mosquitoes, and sometimes we have to deal with angry people who do hurtful things. But we don't have to remain engaged with them. When we say what they did was wrong, it shouldn't have happened, and so on, we are remaining connected with them, staying engaged in the story. Although there might be truth to those sentiments, the more important truth is that we can stop the story right there. This is the same as applying bug spray to protect ourselves against a possible bite. That's all we need to do: protect ourselves so we don't participate in anger.

Using anger or lashing out at other people when we are hurt will not lead to a path of happiness. Rather, we will find ourselves sad. We don't have to have sadness.

Sometimes we will be the ones who make others upset, such as if we accidentally push them, we're late, or we say things that hurt their feelings. We don't act that way intentionally either; we aren't trying to hurt others and are likely unaware of what we've done and how our actions affected others. So if they let us know, perhaps upset with us, we can apologize: "I'm sorry. I didn't mean to do that. I'll try not to do that again."

Of course, we can still engage with people in our loving way, but we have to stop saying that this shouldn't be happening. We have to stop saying this or that is wrong and we have the right to be upset about it. We do have the right to be angry, but it is better to just deal with it. When the mosquito bites, it is going to hurt for five or ten minutes, and then if left it alone, it will pass. If we scratch it, it will irritate us for longer. The same goes for anger. Yes, that person caught us off guard, and we are upset as a result. But we can take a few deep breaths and let it go. Or we can go back home, hug the person we had a fight with, and then move on. It's our minds that keep us angry and hold onto pain. Instead of saying something shouldn't have happened or someone shouldn't have hurt us, all we have to do is say, "Okay, this happened. Now what can I do to protect myself?"

What we tend to do when we stay stuck is to keep thinking about it over and over. That's like scratching the itch continuously. We don't have to do this. When circumstances cause us to feel upset, we can deal with them and move on. When bad things happen to us, we do need to take the time to deal with them as they happen, and then allow ourselves to let them go.

Most of the time when I was out in nature, there would be thousands of mosquitoes all around. I remember once I was camping, and there were so many mosquitoes that I had to run to my tent, diving in so they wouldn't follow me. However, I still enjoyed my time camping. Life is like this sometimes. It can be difficult, but there are still beautiful things we can enjoy about it. If we let our mind create stories about "This shouldn't be happening" or "This angry person shouldn't be doing this" or "This mosquito shouldn't be biting me," we will stay stuck for a very long time until we realize life has mosquitoes.

We can't control everything, but the mosquitoes and angry people don't have to get in the way of our enjoyment of life. Let's just live our lives well and enjoy the beauty that God has given us. Happiness is always ours if we live well right now and keep our minds in the present.

Chapter Twenty
Nine Ways We Can Deal with
Criticism and Find Happiness

When we expose ourselves to other people, we can face criticism, and it can be hard. We all get criticism at some point, and there is no real way to avoid it. But how should we respond—in kind or with kindness?

Recently, I was looking online at a book I wanted to purchase. The author got a very critical review, and he responded to it in kind. Another time, a famous actress was complaining about how cruel and mean critics can be with their comments, particularly about her on the Internet. Unless we never interact with anyone, we can't escape criticism. Sooner or later, we are going to come across people who criticize us. Sadly, in today's age because of the Internet and because people can leave anonymous comments online, they can be cruel; they don't think about the impact their words have on another person. None of us is exempt from it. Every person has the right to his or her opinions, but too often people fail to consider how the recipient might feel. Their words can have devastating impacts on others.

Unfortunately, this happens even with our youth. Some high schoolers have left cruel comments about classmates online. This cyber bullying has resulted in some of the targets committing suicide. So it's not a minor issue; it matters.

Mother Teresa was a very beautiful, angelic person, but she too had people that criticized her, people that didn't like her, and even people that wanted to kill her. So if Mother Teresa can't be liked by everybody, how can we? Let's get over the fact that we cannot be criticized or that if we are so great then everyone will love us. That's not going to happen.

We can still find happiness in our lives, even with the criticisms. Here are eight things we can do to deal with criticism. These suggestions will enable us to deal with it well so we can be happy, because when criticism comes it can cause us to be unhappy.

1. Ignore the Criticism

If we don't know people are criticizing us, then we're not going to feel the criticism. Indeed, ignorance is bliss. If we don't search for criticism, then we're not going to find it or be aware of it. We don't have to look for it from others, and we don't have to create it from within for ourselves. Remember the most critical person is always going to be ourselves. So, if we're not focused on the negative, what was said won't be there, and then ignorance will be blissful for us. Of course, we want to grow and learn, but we don't need to constantly focus on the areas that we know are our weaknesses.

Let me use a simple example. Let's say we have a bald spot at the back of our head, and we're not happy about it. But if we're not looking at it and examining it closely every day, we're not going to be aware of it and won't feel badly about it. We can't do much about it, so why focus on it and be unhappy? The same goes for wrinkles. If we're not examining them closely, we won't notice them and won't feel unhappy about them. Yes, we do get older and get wrinkles, but we don't need to think constantly about them. So too with criticism; we don't need to think about it, and if we don't then we will be able to do better and leave room for happiness.

2. Don't Ask for Criticism

We don't want to ask people what they think about us, particularly if we know they're not going to help us grow from the criticism. Other people can help us learn, but we want ones that are loving and kind and give us instruction to help us improve our behavior. We do not ask for advice from people that are critical no matter what we say or do.

3. Stop Judging

Throughout the day, we might find ourselves judging others. We might see a happy person or a person's colorful dress or a person who is aging in a certain way and have a negative comment. When we judge people, it's not good for them, and it's not good for us. If we do it, we must assume other people are also judging us. Most important, we are going to judge ourselves, too, and we are our harshest critic.

If we stop judging others, then we'll stop judging ourselves and we won't expect others to judge us. We'll no longer look for judgment in their behavior and actions. It's so much easier to think people go about their lives and assume everyone is loving and kind. They might not be happy, but if we assume they are, then that will be our experience. Our minds are incredibly powerful, so whatever we believe is true has great power.

If we stop judging others and we stop judging our lives, we will experience life in a much more beautiful way.

4. Set Boundaries

When our friends criticize us, we need to set boundaries. We can tell them that it hurts our feelings, even though we know they don't mean to do it. Good friends will say that of course they didn't meant to do it and they are very sorry. But if we have friends in our lives that are critical, we have to think if it's good for us to be around them. Is it good for us to be spending time with people that are critical, either of us or other people? Is it healthy? Perhaps we need to find new friends that are loving and kind and spend more time with them and less with our friends who are judgmental towards us or others.

We can also make sure there are good boundaries in other aspects of our life so we are attracting positive influences and keeping out the negative. Boundaries can be set with things we see and hear. If we watch certain shows or listen to music in which people are harsh and critical, it's going to affect us and even condition us. If everything we watch and everyone we hang out with and everything we listen to are loving and kind, those are the things we are going to attract. That's how we will start behaving because we are very much conditioned by things around us. I often sample music—and I'm trying not to be critical of certain music—but the types that are very harsh in meaning are rarely listened to by someone who is in a loving, kind place. They are often listened to by people that are angry and feeling critical and harsh about themselves. We are influenced by people and things around us, so we need to surround ourselves with positive ones.

5. Be Accepting of People's Mistakes

Everyone makes mistakes, but beating up others or ourselves about these failings doesn't help anyone. We need to be gentle with others and ourselves when we make mistakes. With a kinder attitude, we can learn from our errors and more easily do better next time.

If we are critical of mistakes, however, we tend to repeat them because we are thinking about them, bringing attention to them, and becoming afraid of repeating them. The result? We do just that—make the same mistake. Think about children with a very harsh and critical parent. They know they're going to be yelled at if they make the least mistake, such as spill milk. But their fear in slipping up causes so much tension that they invariably do exactly what they are trying to avoid—they spill the milk. Fear, anxiety, and worry are incredibly powerful in causing missteps, but if we start thinking that it's okay to make mistakes and we can learn from them, then life will go better. We will be gentler with ourselves and with other people when mistakes happen.

When we or others make a mistake, we can say, "It's okay to mess up. Now, what can we learn from this?" We accept our fallibility, avoid saying there's something wrong with the one who erred, and put the focus on what we can learn. We then can move forward in a positive way.

6. Understand the Power of Our Thoughts

Thought can have a positive or negative influence, depending upon the nature of the thought. When we steep ourselves in loving thoughts, they can create beautiful, positive changes in us. We start feeling that happiness inside us swell and become who we are. As much as negative thoughts are powerful, so are positive ones. When everything that comes to us is a good thing, we realize everything bad is something we want to stay away from as much as possible. That's a key factor of living a happy life: making sure we surround ourselves with that which is positive because then we are going to experience the love and joy of life. We will be affected by it just as a cup of hot water is permeated by tea leaves. Whatever tea we put in that cup will change the water. What kind of tea will we put in us?

Will it be healthy and good tea or negative tea? Choosing to be as positive and loving as possible will make us positive and loving.

7. Be Loving to Others

When people do things we don't like or we do things they don't like, whose fault is it? We like to blame others. But, really, it's the fault of our conditioning. We have all been conditioned by two very basic things that scientists around the world agree on—our genetics and our environment. Neither one we choose; we're born with our genes, and we are born into and raised in our environment. Even things we think we choose later in life are actually affected by those two things, our genetics and our environment.

By realizing this, we can soften our judgments of ourselves and others. Rarely do people in prison come from beautiful lives, surrounded by love and everything going great with them. However, we can change. Even if we have difficult backgrounds, we can seek out the positive and loving and expose ourselves to things that are good for us and good in our lives. We don't continue to steep in negativity. When we expose ourselves to good conditioning, we get good results; when we expose ourselves to negative things, we get bad results.

We tend to blame people for exposing themselves to negative things, but perhaps we can soften that and realize that we really don't know the whole story. All we know is our own story, and regardless of happened to us, we can begin to be happy. Once we start implementing the changes, we can soften our judgments of others and of ourselves. It might take a little while to learn these points, but we can be softer. It's a lot like going to the gym. If we've never exercised at a gym, it's not going to be easy when we finally do work out. We will get better at it, but it takes time. So too with understanding the effects of conditioning; it takes time. As we learn, we can be gentle with ourselves and others, and stop being so judgmental. If we want to place blame, let's put it on the conditioning and not the person. When we do, our hearts will soften towards others and ourselves.

8. Notice the Negativity Related to Criticism

So many negative thoughts come from hearing criticism of others. If we learn to *be* more and not think so much, when we do hear those criticisms, they won't stick around for long because we will return to just living, living well in the here and now. We'll realize that we are going to have exposure to negativity, but most of what we focus on is in the present moment. If we do that and not keep battling with thoughts of what happened and what people think of us, we will learn to quiet our minds. We will be in the flow of life and in the zone of just loving life, living life well without judgment. Life goes so much better this way.

Chapter Twenty-One
Happiness: Once You Get It, How Do You Keep It Going?

It's wonderful to find more happiness in every day and not to struggle with so much anger or depression. But how do we hold onto this wonderful state?

Through our attachments, we're going to suffer. If we let go of these attachments and work towards living in the present moment, accepting the permanence, watching our mind and having time to be self-loving, then we can find that life becomes easier. But sometimes after people find that happiness, they forget or revert to old ways. They stop looking after themselves, and then after a while, they can't figure out why their lives aren't working anymore.

We get out of emotional health.

To stay in top physical condition, we know what to do. Even the best athletes will get out of shape if they stop exercising and eating well. It's the same with happiness. In order to maintain, there are things we must do.

Although happiness is a natural state, there are a lot of things that can block it. It's like eating well. If we eat only food that is super healthy, organic, and fresh, we get in a great habit of eating well every day. However, the messages we receive in the world are that we should be eating fast food or processed foods. Pressure and temptation surrounds us telling us to abandon our good intentions. The world is like that. It's not going to encourage us to take care of ourselves and be happy. The world is going to do just the opposite.

In fact, the world constantly bombards us with messages to make bad decisions: "Be attached! Suffer! Indulge yourself! Have addictions. Crave the unhealthy." When we choose to live in the present moment without attachments, the world is going to say, "No! You need that new car. No! You're going to suffer if you don't get that great job. No! Things are going to go wrong if you're always physically healthy." Much of the world is going to fight against us being happy.

But the good news is we can maintain our state of happiness and continue to improve it if we do certain things.

Everything Matters

First, we have to acknowledge that everything we do matters. We are not going to reach a point where our actions or thoughts have no effect. This is true for everything—the little and the significant. If we often eat rich desserts, we will compromise our health. If we skip exercising one day, we will justify doing that several days a week, and then just won't bother at all.

When we do things that we acknowledge aren't the best for us, that we know are going against what keeps us healthy and happy, then we have to say, "Okay! I acknowledge this. I'm not going to be immune to this, so I am going to do it in little doses. In that way, I won't get addicted to it and fall into a trap of thinking I am so mighty that nothing will impact me." That's what gets everyone in the long run—they think they're above things like that. But we are affected by our choices and what we expose ourselves to. When we acknowledge that and say, "We're all human. Anyone can fall from grace," then we're going to be far more careful.

If I'm walking on ice and know it, I'm going to be a lot more careful than if I am walking on cement. If we are careful and we surround ourselves with good things and avoid the things that aren't good for us, we're going to do well in life. But we're not going to do well if we think we have reached a certain point where it doesn't matter and now can do whatever we want. That's almost a guarantee to crash and burn. So let's acknowledge that we are human and we are going to be affected by the things that are negative. Let's limit ourselves when it comes to these negative things.

Continue Doing What Works

Second, if we discovered what keeps us happy in a healthy way, we need to keep doing it. In the same way, if we exercise and then see we stay in shape, we keep exercising. We don't expect to stay healthy by abandoning our exercise program. Just as we're going to get out of shape if we don't exercise, we can get out of happiness shape if we don't focus on it.

Sometimes, we forget what not being happy feels like. We might think, "Oh. it's just so boring being happy. I want a little excitement, some drama." Some people do create turmoil in their lives just for the variety. This may sound funny if you're not happy and wanting to be. But once they drop into the drama they've created, they remember why they wanted happiness instead. It's a roller coaster ride and not nearly as satisfying as staying happy and enjoying that state.

I knew a wonderful woman who had been in abusive situation but turned her life around. She became a speaker for women that were in domestic violence situations and did a lot of work with shelters. There she saw something similar to the drama-happiness roller coaster. When a woman arrived in the shelter, at first, she would be so relieved to be out of the violent situation because it had been so frightening and scary for her. But after a few days, the woman would get bored, go to a nearby bar, and start engaging in risky behavior because she was restless. It was almost as if the experience in the shelter was too peaceful that it became boring.

We have to be careful about throwing away our happiness for drama that will harm us. Once we have found happiness, we don't have to abandon excitement. We leave behind only the kind that hurts us; healthy excitement we create and welcome.

We stay with the happiness and keep doing things that have been working in the past. If we know things that are good, we should make sure they are a part of our daily experiences. If have a friend who is always positive and loving, we call or visit her now and then. If we spend time in nature and the experience always revitalizes us, then we repeat that. We keep doing what works, what keeps us on the right path. If we keep doing these things, they are going to help us stay in happiness shape.

Routines help us stay on track. But if they are new, we have to take time to make them part of our life. Once we establish them, they're great at keeping us in happiness shape. Boredom might kick in, but remember that's just the ego trying to trick us into letting go. We can have beautiful lives, and it's much easier to do that if we have routines. One of the routines I find helpful is meditation. Typically, I meditate twice a day, usually half an hour to forty-five minutes each session. I love doing it, and I find it's a healthy routine for me.

Deep in ourselves are the things that put a smile on our face and help us accept what is and ultimately love what is. We delve into our depths, discover what brings us true happiness, and live beautiful lives. But unless we keep working at keeping this happiness state, it's not going to stay there. We have to be careful and make sure that the things we learn we continually put into practice.

Live in the Moment

Sometimes we think of what we are doing and don't feel we can do it for the rest of our lives. Today we can do it, but we're not sure about every day of our future. Those future days don't matter right now. All that does is this moment.

If we can do it for today, we probably can do it tomorrow and the day after and so on. But all we need worry about is if we can do it today. Can we? The answer is going to be, "Yes, I can do it today." Can you maintain it? No idea. But each morning when we wake up, we can say, "Can I keep doing these things today? Yup! I can." Then all those days are going to add up to a beautiful life.

This is what helps me maintain things—concentrating on doing them only in this moment. No matter what life throws at us, we stay in a place where we will be okay. We land on our feet, and we keep coming back to that state of peacefulness and happiness.

It's just too overwhelming to think about doing this for years and years to come. If we do take it one day at a time, it magically does evolve into a beautiful life. We can handle almost anything one day at a time. So let's live in that present moment of "Yes, I know it works. I get it now. I'm going to keep doing what I do to make myself a happy, healthy, whole person today." The next day we will commit again. It's beautiful when we can apply that and it works.

And if we do falter? It's not so overwhelming. We just say, "Oops! Fell off the horse. Need to get back on." That's what we do. We're always gentle when we mess up. Everyone does at some point, but we just get back on and say, "Yup! Today I can do this." It's much easier when we do take it one day at a time.

Recap

Can we maintain happiness? Yes! So, how do we do it? We have to do three things.

1. We acknowledge that we can lose that happiness and so we will be careful to make sure we keep it.
2. We keep doing things that work and establish routines that almost force us to get into a positive habit.
3. We stay in the moment and worry only about maintaining our happiness one day at a time, which turns into a lifetime of happiness.

Chapter Twenty-Two
How to Lose Sadness and Find Happiness

Almost twenty years ago, the most wonderful event happened to me. At a local pet store, I saw a beautiful yellow Labrador retriever for sale. I immediately took him home and named him Einstein. Einstein was a magnificent dog, the smartest dog I ever knew. I had the privilege of taking him to work with me every single day. He would be with me while I worked with my patients, and he would help them when they were feeling sad. He had a real sensitivity to people and their emotions, going to them and kissing them when they were feeling down. Einstein was a great companion, and we did a lot of hiking together. For fifteen and a half years, he was with me almost every single day.

If you are a pet or people lover, you know how attached we can become to a person or animal with whom we spend a whole lifetime. We love them, they return that love, and we form a tight loving bond.

Well, after fifteen and a half years, Einstein finally came to his end, and thankfully I was with him when he died. When he took his last breath and he was gone, tears just flowed out of me. Already I missed him, and I was so very sad about his passing.

The sadness did dissipate, and I slowly felt better. But at moments, I still felt a wave of sorrow pass over me. Each time I needed to cry, I allowed myself that time to cry, and then I would feel better. When I miss him now, I am not sad anymore; rather, I am glad for the valuable time I had with him.

My grandmother also loved animals, and when the last dog she had passed away, she said, "I'm never gonna get a dog again; it's just too hard to lose them." I think this is what a lot of us do in life. We have sad experiences happen to us, and they are just too hard, and we don't want them ever to happen again. So, we put up our walls and do things that prevent us from feeling pain. What we don't realize is that by trying to prevent pain, we also block happiness.

So how can we experience the sadness of life and still live a happy life? How can we be happy with sadness? Sadness is actually a very healthy emotional response to events that happen to us, and we all will likely experience sadness of some sort in life. We're going to have losses, and if we feel those losses, they can help us move forward. Things are impermanent, things change, we feel them, and the natural, healthy response to change is sadness and tears. It's normal, and it's healthy for us.

Unfortunately, many of us transform that sadness into depression, which keeps us stuck.

Sadness and shedding tears for a loss are normal and healthy. But when we think those sad feelings will be with us forever and we will never be happy again or an experience was so horrible that it shouldn't have happened, we step out of sadness and move into depression. There is nothing wrong with being sad, but we have to be careful that it doesn't turn into depression. Once depression kicks in, we can feel horrible and at the end of that crying session we're not going to feel better.

This is something important to look out for. Is our time of being sad helping us to feel better or not? To keep sadness from overwhelming us or turning into depression, we have to limit our sorrow to only moments. If, instead, we're thinking about what's causing our sadness over and over, it's going to turn it into depression. If we don't want to be depressed and we do want to be happy, then we need to be sad when we're sad but then continue to live because life isn't about loss. Yes, we sometimes experience loss, and sometimes a loss can be horrible. But life isn't only about that; in life there will always be beautiful things going on.

To be happy, we need to learn to live in the present time. In the moment right now, life isn't pure sadness; it never is. There might be different types of sadness, but not pure sadness.

Our lives are filled with stories. But sometimes, we get caught up in one. We stay stuck with it, playing it over in our minds. We're no longer in the moment because that story is about what happened before; it's not happening now. Replaying the story may make us feel good if it is a good story. But guess what? That good story is going to pass. If it's a bad story, it's also going to pass if we let it. Stories pass over us all the time, unless our mind keeps feeding them to us.

So what we can do instead is learn to be with what is. What's happening right now? If you're out with your friends and having a good time, have a good time and know that you don't need to feel depressed.

Some people experience a great loss and think they have to be sad to honor the memory, for instance, of a loved one who passed away. We think we *have to be sad*. We don't have to be—it's a choice. But the choice to look out for isn't the sadness but is allowing or not allowing the sadness to turn into depression. Depression is based on thoughts, and we don't need to be so caught up in all our thoughts. We can prevent them from getting in the way of our living life well.

The key is to live in the present moment. If right now we feel the urge to cry, then that's fine. At the end of the sad crying session, we should feel better. The crying is over, the sadness has passed, and we can continue living our day and get back to living life. It's about staying out of our heads, letting go of thoughts from the past, and staying in the present moment. When we do that, we can have a beautiful life because in the present moment there will always be something beautiful. If we choose to be with the beauty and not get stuck with the loss in the pain or in the attachments to that loss, we remember that life is impermanent and so we don't have to suffer. We say, "Oh, here comes that story again. Instead, I need to get back to what's happening here now." Whenever that story comes, we just focus on what is happening *now*. With time and practice, we'll get better at this, and we will train ourselves to be happy.

Yes, there is going to be sadness, and there is nothing wrong with it. But it should take up only a small part of our lives, not large chunks of it. Most of our lives can be beautiful if we just allow ourselves to live in the present moment, live life, and enjoy what we have.

Chapter Twenty-Three
From Fear to Happiness in Four Steps

Fear, anxiety, and stress too often keep us from being happy. But we don't need to let them have such influence over us. We can reclaim our rightful happiness. Before giving the four steps to help, let's look at what fear is all about.

Fears can manifest in many different ways. For example, we can be sleeping, relaxing, or having a good time, and then all of a sudden a thought comes. We let the thought grow, feed it, and it turns into fear. That causes suffering and takes away from our happiness. Later, perhaps we are driving, spending time with our friends, or doing our daily activities, and that thought returns, paralyzing us. It causes us not to be happy or enjoy happiness as our natural state.

Fear comes up when some of our negative thoughts permeate our lives and cause us to suffer. They stem from attachments. Perhaps we're fearful because we attach to certain outcomes and we don't want certain things to happen. For example, I was very blessed to live with my mother's mother for three years when I was in college. My grandmother was a very beautiful, loving, caring person whom I deeply loved and grew to know well during those years. But sadly, a few years later, she developed dementia and Alzheimer's disease. Though she lived for another ten years, slowly her mind started to go, until she didn't recognize anyone at the end of her life.

After she died, I was talking with my mother and sensed something was wrong. I asked her what was bothering her, and she confessed that she was afraid of getting Alzheimer's as her mother had. Unfortunately, she also got it and passed away. But the saddest part was her fear, which affected her life before she suffered from the disease. She was so afraid that she couldn't enjoy her good life then.

Fear has huge effects on our lives. When we are fearful, we are not living well. Whatever we are afraid of keeps us from enjoying the here and now.

We can also let what we fear become reality by thinking about it too much. By encouraging thoughts about what might happen, we focus on that scenario, look for, and develop a self-fulfilling prophecy where what we think about tends to become a reality.

Although it's good to have basic fears in place so that we don't do silly things that can harm us or others, we don't need to keep thinking about fears once we know what to be careful of. We don't keep thinking, "If I drive 120 miles per hour, I'm really going to get into an accident." We just drive responsibly and let that fear-inducing thought go.

With other fears that are not so easily dismissed, we tend to try to solve the problem behind the fear by thinking about it over and over. It's like pouring gasoline over a fire. It isn't helping because we are just feeding the fear and getting nowhere. When we constantly think about the same things, the fear can become paralyzing. More important, it keeps us from living well here and now because when we are fearful we are not focused on life that is happening in the moment.

It is therefore important to realize that our thoughts are powerful and often even more powerful than what we are afraid of because by thinking about it, it contributes to our stress. That is needless suffering. Often the fears we have never become true, but we suffer so much because we keep thinking, "What if they do?" It's those thoughts that stop us from living in the present moment.

By having those thoughts of being afraid, we miss out on happiness in our life because we spend so much time being afraid. We can be on vacation having a great time, but spending half the holiday worried about how much money we're spending, worried about our flights being on time, worried about our animals being okay back home. And all the worrying only takes away from the enjoyment of our vacation.

Here is another thing that I often see. People's lives are going well—they have good relationships with their spouses, their kids are doing well, and their finances are in a good place. But they still end up being fearful. I then figure out that they spend a large amount of time watching the news, which focuses on tragedy, terror, and fearful events, and this is causing them a lot of stress and anxiety. When they stop watching so much of the news, they do better. They no longer have the graphic scenes making them feel needlessly afraid

Our thoughts are very powerful. What we think can bring misery into our lives or great joy, regardless of our circumstance. For example, if our doctor says we have cancer and have to have radiation and chemotherapy treatment, we can react in various ways. We might say, "Okay, the doctor told me what to do." This is not going to be fun, but we will deal with it, enjoy ourselves, and not think of disappointment. Or we might react in a very different way. We might start worrying about losing our hair or being in pain or not even surviving the treatment, all before anything happens. We would be suffering not from the cancer or the treatment but because of our fears.

So how do we keep the power of fear from overwhelming us? What can we do when faced with fear? Here are four steps to take us out of fear and return to happiness.

1. Release Judgment

When a fear arises, first we must not criticize ourselves for having it. Our fears come from various places, and nothing good is going to come up from criticizing ourselves for having those fears. The fears are there. We don't judge ourselves but just notice the fear.

2. Address the Fear in a Positive Way

We face our fear and figure out how to deal with it. For example, if we fear losing our job because the company is downsizing, we think about what we can do right now to lessen the fear. We can search for jobs on the Internet, start brainstorming for job opportunities we hadn't considered before, and talk to different people about different jobs that could be options for us. We can investigate going to school, taking classes, and furthering our education.

3. Know You Will Be Okay

We can also face the situation and ask a simple question, "Am I going to be okay?" Yes, what we fear can be hard to confront, but we can deal with them, no matter how horrific they are, like death, divorce, or losing our jobs. Our fears keep us from living well right now. Our fear of dying prevents us from living now; our fear of divorce keep us from loving well now; our fear of losing our job keeps us from enjoying the present time well and being productive at work. So it's better if we can say, "Yes, I do not want what is behind this fear to happen, but if it does, I'll be okay. No matter what, I'll be okay." If we want to be happy, we say it and believe it.

Happiness is an unconditional state—it doesn't depend on getting or having anything. We can't say, "I need this or that to be happy." Instead, we say, "I live well. I love well," and then happiness arises. Any attachment that we have will keep us from being happy. Letting go of attachments doesn't mean we can't pursue things or can't love things. We can but without being attached to them. We are going to do a lot better if we are able to face our fears and say, "Of course I don't want this fearful event to happen, but if it does, I'll be okay."

4. Be in the Moment

To move from fear to happiness, we need to live well now, love well now, and focus on what's happening right now. Think about what you could do right now that would be fun. Just enjoy the power and presence of now because in the now there are no fears. When our minds are still, there is no fear. Fears come from thoughts, but in the now, they don't exist. So what we can do is very simply find something to be with right now. Fears need thoughts. If we can work towards quietening our minds, stilling those thoughts, and just being present with what is, life goes so much better. Accept what is, love what is because when we love what is, there is no fear.

Recap

We don't have to stay stuck in fear. We can move into happiness with four steps.

1. Release judgment. Don't judge yourself for having fears
2. Address the fear in a positive way. See if there's anything you can do for your fears right now.
3. Know you will be okay. Ask yourself how you would manage if your fears did become a reality and know that you would be okay.
4. Be in the moment. Live well now instead of focusing on the fear.

Don't feel the fear. We'll find that we will naturally melt into happiness, and that will become our natural state because we won't be feeding our fears with our thoughts. As we do that, we get better. As we take care of things proactively and live life well instead of in a fearful way, we'll find that we can have the most beautiful life imaginable, even beyond our imagination because it is beyond the mind.

Chapter Twenty-Four
Agathism—
The Best Way to Live Our Lives

A few years ago, I was driving a Toyota Forerunner that had been in my possession for more than fourteen years. It had 274,000 miles on the odometer, and it was still running, although, of course, not perfectly. I finally decided I needed a new car, and since I tend to keep the vehicles that I buy for so long, I was determined to get exactly what I wanted. A new hybrid that I had been reading about had piqued my interest, and I decided that this was what I would purchase. Unfortunately, my plans were dashed because the particular hybrid I wanted wouldn't be available for a couple more years. I ultimately decided to lease a car, more than willing to wait to get what I wanted.

If you know anything about car leases, you know that you're not supposed to put too many miles on the leased vehicle. Since I had a fairly lengthy commute back and forth from work; putting a substantial number of miles on my lease was inevitable.

Towards the end of the contract, I let someone drive a car that was in my name, too. Since this person drove short distances every day it would not add significant mileage to the car. Just before my leased car was due to be returned, this person had a car accident, hitting another car and damaging both vehicles.

This person and I could have had an argument. We could have been angry at one another and fought about the extra cost of fixing the leased car and the other car. This incident could have kept us from being happy, but it didn't. We felt disappointed, of course, but a little disappointment happens in life. We realized this, and thus we were able to move forward.

There is a powerful message to this little anecdote. Bad things sometimes occur in life, and we have three choices regarding how to address them.

Choice number one is to be pessimistic, negative, and upset. Many people choose this path and dwell on the negativity. Choosing this path makes people feel sad and unhappy and can lead to an unsuccessful life. Obviously, I do not recommend taking this approach.

A second choice is to be optimistic; we can believe that everything will be well and deem everything to be great and wonderful. This course of action is, obviously, a much better approach for our mental health than negativity and pessimism. Optimism helps us to look at events in a brighter, more positive way. However, the danger of being optimistic is that we often don't sufficiently deal with our feelings. If we are overly optimistic, we risk taking an unreal approach and pushing away our true feelings before they are adequately addressed.

It is entirely appropriate that when something bad happens, we feel it. When the leased car was wrecked, of course I felt disappointed and even a little angry. I didn't want to spend the money to have it fixed, but that's what had to happen. I allowed myself to feel upset, but I dealt with my emotions and realized that I had to let go of any lingering negativity.

A third choice in dealing with life's unfortunate occurrences, and the way I recommend we live life, is to take an agathist approach. An agathist is someone who believes that in the long run, even though bad things sometimes happen, everything will eventually work out for the best.

Returning to my car leasing example, I certainly wasn't happy about having to repair the car after the accident, but I dealt with my emotions and let them go. And in the end, everything turned out pretty well.

With regard to happiness, taking an agathistic approach is a great way to live. We agathists fully experience our emotions, always remaining kind toward others. After the troublesome event has passed, we watch calmly as things mostly turn out well. As long as we keep an agathistic approach to living, we learn lessons and we grow. By expecting that things will ultimately turn out well, they often do.

Agathism doesn't negate our bad experiences. The death of a child, a contentious divorce, a traumatic accident, and other unfortunate events do occur. We all experience hardship or loss, some more extreme than others. But agathism looks beyond the trauma and knows better will come. When something bad happens, it doesn't mean that life is over, or that we should resign ourselves to giving up. We must hang in there, remembering that it is always the darkest just before the dawn. The sun will surely rise, and things will begin to get better.

There is a woman with whom I have worked in my practice who had a severely challenging life. Think of the most awful horror movie you can—she lived through worse and had to keep living it. After our working together, now she is one of the wisest, most internally beautiful people I have ever met. She would agree that her life has turned out very well in the end. She has incredible faith; she is very deep and reaches out to so many people in the world with her story in order to share her growth, her success, and her journey of overcoming her very, very dark life.

Keep in mind that the way in which we think about things matters. Of course, part of our goal is to live in the present moment and simply enjoy the journey. But when we are experiencing tough times, we need to remember to not give up, to have hope, and to believe that in the long run things can turn out well; this is the way in which we need to approach life. We simply hang in there and don't give up.

My client who led such a horrible life would have never achieved such great wisdom and such a keen ability to reach out to so many other people had she not lived through her dark experiences. Don't get me wrong: I do not wish for us to experience terrible things. Of course, I want all of us to live very happy lives. But when bad things happen, as they will to the vast majority of us, we must remember to take an agathistic approach. Believe that in the end negative events may actually turn into something good. Be open to the possibility that there may be a lesson to learn, an opportunity for growth, or an unexpected positive outcome.

An agathistic approach to life allows us to be true to our emotions, to experience them, and not to deny they exist. It is good to experience our feelings and to live our lives. Indeed, we must do both, and the agathist approach helps us accomplish this. Living in the present moment, no matter how tough times are, is surely a great way to live. No matter how challenging life can be, we must remember that there is always something beautiful toward which we can look forward.

Chapter Twenty-Five
The Happiness Recipe:
Throw in Adaptation

Life is amazing. It has ups and downs, successes and failures, joys and sorrows, bliss and agony. Life has many different aspects to it, but despite our efforts to control it, life is sometimes quite unpredictable. We just don't know how events are going to turn out. We can work hard trying to figure them out and preparing for them. But no matter how hard we try, sometimes life changes the course we're on. Sometimes, it does so quite shockingly. We may invest time and money in acquiring a specific skill, decades devoted to a marriage, tremendous effort in raising children, and then things change. New technology replaces our skills; our marriages end; our children get sick and die. Life doesn't always go the way we expect it to. Why don't things go our way after all our hard work?

It's actually quite simple. Like the weather, life has so many factors that influence it that we can't predict what will happen more than a few hours into the future, if even that. We are as complex as the weather—actually more so. The weather deals just with the environment. When it comes to predicting our future, we have two major factors involved—our self and our environment.

The first, our self, doesn't stay the same our entire life. Our preferences change—where we like to live, what we like to do, foods we like to eat, and more.

As we grow up, we're exposed to so much in our environment that affects us and over which we have no control. We might choose a partner for marriage, but that person can change and no longer share our goals or aspirations. We might choose a city to live in, but economic factors beyond our influence can create a recession so we lose our job. There are just too many factors that play into our future for us to be very good at predicting them. None of us can predict when we're coming home at night from a movie if a drunk driver is going to kill us. None of us knows how long we will live. Young adults and even children get cancer and die suddenly.

Despite the difficulty in making accurate predictions, we keep trying. It's okay to try, but we stumble when we get caught in believing things must turn out the way we predicted. We have high expectations that events must turn out in a certain way, and the second we do, we set ourselves up for failure because things so often change. Many things change, and we don't know what they are or how they will influence the outcome. So if we hang on tightly and say a situation *has* to be this way and then it doesn't, we are going to suffer.

For instance, I have a friend who drives like a maniac and has always been quite proud of his speeding. For ten years, he astoundingly never got a speeding ticket. I thought it wouldn't last if he kept driving that way, and sure enough, in one year, he got three tickets in a row. He had made a prediction that if he drove in a certain way, he would be okay and everything would work out fine. Life said something different: "Listen up! Here are three fines." Fortunately, he let go of his expectation that he could drive how he wanted. He realized he had to slow down or else risk losing his license.

We all know people whose lives seem perfect. Everything turns out perfectly for them

And then, there are the rest of us. We think that if we get a good job and work hard, then everything will turn out great. But it's probably not going to happen that way. We're going to make plans for the future, be excited about them, and some of them are going to turn out. But many of them are not. That's a critical point. If we're like my friend, driving crazily and thinking he's not going to get a ticket, sooner or later, we will get into trouble. If we think, "Oh, I know what's going to happen in my life, and things will work out perfectly," we'll probably get some rude awakenings. We're fighting a natural law—we're trying to go against the inevitable.

Sometimes we go for a year of smooth sailing, and then all of a sudden the winds shift so rapidly, and we're caught off guard. We need to get to the state of saying, "Okay, I get it. Life changes. So how do I do well with these changes?"

It's actually very simple. If we accept the fact that life changes, then when it does, we can just adapt to it. We don't fight it. We don't scream about it. We don't say, "This is unfair." Rather, we say, "Oh! A change!" The mere fact that we accept and acknowledge the change helps us.

Then we say, "Okay, this is the change. How do I live well with this new situation?" We don't fight it. We don't say, "This shouldn't have happened. It's unfair. I don't get it." That attitude causes suffering. What helps is to excel with the change and we can do that just by accepting it. We ask, "How do I make this new state I'm facing as beautiful as possible? How do I make this new experience wonderful?" Maybe we've lost a job and now have six months so can go back to school. Maybe our partner has walked out so we have the opportunity to find a better mate, someone more compatible. Maybe I have cancer right now so I have the opportunity to grow emotionally and spiritually, because I really haven't been doing that.

Anything life throws at us can be something that can make our lives better. This is not a flippant remark because I work with people that have very dark tragedies and they do exactly what I'm saying here. And I see the same effect wherever I go. I love traveling the world and meeting people. When I encounter people doing well with life, in an excellent place, although they might not be wealthy or successful I ask them, "What got you here? How are you in this place emotionally where life is going well for you?" And I always get the same answer: "Suffering got me here. I was tired of suffering so I learned how to get better with life."

This is one of the key factors that help us live better with life. When we adapt, we're going to say, "Okay, life, you always have lessons to teach me. What are the lessons this time? I'm here to learn them." With that attitude—the ability to adapt well to whatever life gives us—we can say, "Yup. This is what I have. I'm gonna make this work, whatever it is." Then life is going to go great. It really is because now, instead of fighting life, we flow with life. When we flow with it, no matter what it is, it will work out.

As long as there is one person that has done well with a story that we are going through, then it's a possibility for us and anyone else. We all know of people whose lives have been quite tragic but turned out to be beautiful. We can be one of them too if we choose to adapt well to life.

So whenever we face a new challenge, here's what we can do. First, we say, "Is there anything I can do to make this better?" Ask that, but don't overexert yourself with answers. We tend to do it too much and overthink and exhaust ourselves.

Next, we ask, "How do I adapt to this change?" This involves *really* accepting that this is the way it's going to go now and adapting to it. Period.

Let me use an example to illustrate this point. Years ago, I was flying back from France with a friend. We'd been there for a couple of weeks exploring the country together, and on our way home, we were both really tired. We arrived in New York City for our last flight home, but our flight was delayed by eight hours. So we had several options available to us. We could wait use the eight hours to explore the city. I like New York City, so I found transport and had a nice time doing just that. My friend took a different option. He was upset with the airlines for the delay and just stayed in the terminal fighting, fuming, and being upset. When I came back after enjoying the city, he was still upset. We both got home eventually. But I got home relaxed because I accepted the fact the flight was delayed.

Now, I'm not judging him. I am using this situation as an example of how we have choices in life—we can fight or we can flow; we can fume about the change we don't like or we can adapt to them. Life throws us things that we do not expect to happen. After we have exhausted everything we can think of to make it better right now or maybe later and we reach a point where there is nothing left that we can do, then we adapt and just love life.

So here's another example. Imagine we're lying in bed and worrying about various things. We can ask ourselves, "Is there anything we can do at three o'clock in the morning to rectify this situation?" And if there isn't, then we can say, "Well, I'm not tired, so perhaps I'll listen to some music and see if I fall back to sleep. If I don't, I don't. If I do, I do." We're not fighting the situation, stressing or getting worked up, which can make whatever is worrying us even worse.

We can really do well when we adapt to life instead of fighting it. Let's try it—we're certainly going to have plenty of opportunities when things don't turn out the way we want them to. So instead of fighting the situation, let's figure out how we can adapt to it instead. Let's make what is happening something better. We really don't have to fight so hard. After we've done what we can to make things better, we move on to the next step and just live and live well. We are very capable of it.

Instead of trying to force life to follow a path we have set, we can adapt to changes and have great lives, no matter what the Universe throws at us.

Chapter Twenty-Six
Deal with the Pain, Breathe, and
Get Back on the Horse

Once a quarter, I go to a beautiful retreat center in Santa Barbara to rejuvenate and just have a very peaceful and quiet weekend. The last time I was there, they had signs posted everywhere and they told us in person that there is a severe drought in Santa Barbara so we have to be very careful not to use too much water.

I said to them, "I thought Santa Barbara built a desalinization plant." They said the city had started to but when the water shortage wasn't such a crisis anymore they stopped building it. Now of course they're building it again because they need the water; however, it is delayed and will take a few more years to finish. By the time they get close to finishing it, the water shortage may be gone again.

We can laugh at this and say how silly. They should just prepare for the inevitable, finish what they start, and get it done. Seems simple, doesn't it? But we don't do much better, unfortunately. We expect things to stay the same, and when they don't, we have trouble.

It really is a fact of life and nature that things change, and unfortunately we're very seldom prepared for them. We get stuck because we think everything's going to stay the same; whatever's going on now is going to continue. We especially think this when things are going well. We all know that it won't. Why do we think that things will stay the same when we absolutely know they won't? It comes down to a very simple concept—attachment. We're attached to keeping things the way they are; we don't want them to change. But life does change.

So how do we live in this life of impermanence? How do we live well knowing that things are going to change?

There are three things we can do to live well with impermanence.

1. We can accept that life is impermanent and things are going to change.
2. We can prepare for the change because it is going to happen.
3. When the change comes, we can deal with it in the moment, and then we can move on.

Let me use an example to illustrate this. Recently I had a special deal to go horseback riding with my children. I'm not a horse expert, but I grew up riding horses, and my children had ridden a little bit too, so we were all very excited. When we got there, the woman who was our guide had our horses ready. We climbed onto them, and she gave us some instructions. At one point, we were climbing a steep embankment and going faster and faster. All of a sudden, my saddle twisted off to the side, and off I went from the horse to the ground, falling on my back and landing on two very sharp rocks that dug into my back. I rolled over and just lay there. I was in so much pain I couldn't move; the only thing I could do was breathe. So I breathed deeply, and in about three minutes, I started to be able to move. I got up, adjusted the saddle, and got back on my horse, and we finished the ride. When I got home, the pain continued, so the next morning, I went to urgent care where they took some X-rays and found nothing was broken. They gave me painkillers so I could sleep at night, and for about three days, I took those painkillers, and they helped me.

So, let's go over this situation by looking at the three points of dealing with impermanence.

The first is accepting that life is full of change. When I got on the horse, I wasn't expecting to fall off and be in excruciating pain, but I know if I live long enough sometimes that's going to happen; sometimes I'm going to get hurt. Thankfully, I didn't break my back or hit my head, but I was in a lot of pain, and I dealt with that pain, realizing that this does sometimes happen. I didn't create stories like, "Why did this happen to me? Why didn't the guide put the saddle on tight enough?" All I could do was deal with the pain, breathe, and then get back on the horse. So the first thing we have to do is accept that life does change and sometimes that change is quite unpleasant. It can even result in physical pain, as it did for me. But we don't have to suffer in resisting that change.

The second part is preparing for a change. Here's the part that I didn't do: even though I had my kids wearing helmets, I wasn't wearing one. If my head had landed just a few inches in a different place, I wouldn't be writing this right now. I know we make mistakes sometimes, and we can't prepare for everything. Sometimes we do silly things. I was doing a silly thing by not wearing a helmet. So we can prepare, but we can't prepare for everything.

The next thing we have to do is deal with it. In my situation, when I was in excruciating pain, I had to focus on the pain rather than on why this happened to me. The latter is actually the suffering part of it—the story we create about what's happening. I was just in pain and breathing to lessen the pain so I could get up, and that's all it took. I've learned that if I breathe very deeply and slowly the pain subsides, and it did thankfully.

After the ride, I continued to deal with it. I made some phone calls, saw the doctor, and had some X-rays. Then I made some appointments with a chiropractor, and since that time I've been getting better without creating any stories or beating myself up for falling off the horse or not preparing well enough or not checking the saddle.

So let's review. Impermanence is a natural part of our life; change is inevitable. If we fight reality, we'll suffer because life is going to change, no matter what. We might think we'll change it, but it will change us. We accept that life is going to change. Just accepting that it will change will position us for the following step.

Next, we prepare for change. We think about how everything we have—our loved ones, our health, our money, whatever we hang onto—can change. If we are prepared for the fact that it may be taken from us someday, we can be ready for it. We have to be willful of being prepared for that change because, in one form or another—we are all going to die—it will happen.

A good way to prepare for it is to write down things we're attached to and say, "When X is taken away from me, I'll be really sad," and then imagine X being taken away. Of course, we don't want this to happen, and we don't dwell on it. But because it might, we think about how we would prepare for it.

The last point is to deal with the circumstance when it happens, instead of creating stories around it, such as "it shouldn't have been this way," or "it shouldn't have happened to me." Is it better that other people suffer and we don't? We may want that, but we may suffer sometimes too. We are going to go through painful events and need to deal with them, heal from them, and move forward so we will be better. One of the great things about just dealing with things when they happen is that we realize this may not be a big deal and we don't have to spend so much energy focusing on it. When we go through a tragedy or experience suffering, we tend to give a lot of attention to it, and we don't have to do that. Remember, on my horseback ride, I got back on the horse and continued the ride.

There is always something beautiful to be with. What our mind focuses on is what we're going be with, so why not be with something besides the physical pain or the suffering that we're going through? When we're distracted, we will feel better. We don't always have to be with our suffering; there's always something else we can be with. A prisoner can focus on something other than the sentence and prison conditions; a person in the hospital can focus on something other than the pain; someone going through a divorce can think about something other than the settlement. We can do many other things, and we'll realize with time as we get better that we're not thinking about that loss anymore. That's actually how we get better: we stop thinking about it and start being present and loving what is right now.

So to recap, life is impermanent; it's going to change. There are three ways we can deal with it: one, accept that life is impermanent; two, prepare for that impermanence; and three, when it happens, deal with it, and deal with it well.

Chapter Twenty-Seven
How Our Enemies Can Be Our Teachers

When I was young, I was very impatient with other drivers. I thought they were rude, disrespectful, and posed a challenge for me. Then one Christmas when I was in graduate school, something happened to me that told me I was the one who needed to change.

I was at the mall buying some gifts for family and friends. In the parking lot, a car pulled out right in front of me, and I had to slam on my brakes in order not to hit it. The car's driver had to stop immediately after pulling out in front of me because of the heavy traffic, and so I got out of my car to talk to him about what had happened. He immediately rolled up his windows and locked his car. He wouldn't even look at me! I was so upset and frustrated with him that I banged on the top of his car with my fist hard enough to put a dent in it. I realized later that this man was actually afraid of me and that I needed to change. The other drivers were making me too upset and it wasn't good for me or for them.

What did I do to change myself? I drove with other people who didn't get upset when they were driving. I realized that the other drivers were my teachers. They were driving as they normally drove, and I was upset because there was something wrong with me. I was the one who needed to change! I realized that when I am in a hurry, as I was this particular day during the Christmas season, I am impatient. If I slow down, I am much more patient. I learned that by slowing down and trying not to be in a hurry by giving myself lots of extra time, all of a sudden, the other drivers didn't seem rude anymore. I stopped experiencing rude drivers. That man at the mall and all the other rude drivers I had experienced ended up being my teachers. They had something to tell me about myself, and when I learned my lesson, my feelings of upset went away.

Now I live in Southern California where many people feel there are lots of rude drivers, but I don't feel that way at all. I enjoy driving, always allowing myself plenty of time to get to where I'm going, and I really don't experience rude drivers. I'm not pretending; I honestly don't experience them. I know they exist because sometimes when others are riding with me they'll say, "Oh! Did you see that? How rude that driver was!" But I just don't experience it. Sometimes I think, "Well, that person's in a hurry" or "Something must be wrong." Most of the time, however, I don't even notice them.

I learned that when someone else makes me upset, that person isn't actually causing my emotions; rather, the upset feelings are within me. If I change me, then my upset feelings disappear.

This relates to a special rule of science. Science states that if one person is able to resist getting upset about something, then it is a possibility for all. Here is a personal example. Many years ago, one of my loved ones was diagnosed with cancer, and he passed away four and a half years later. Before his death, he would tell people that those last years were the best of his entire life. He enjoyed his family, he connected with people, and he learned to live to the fullest, even when facing the pain of cancer. Perhaps we can all think of someone we know who is struggling with a physical ailment and is doing well. As long as there is one person out there who is able to do this, then it's a possibility for all of us.

What keeps us from celebrating life and being happy is not our circumstances but us. If we change the way we see things, we can be happy, no matter what. This doesn't mean we're not going to do things to change or make our situation better, but when we've done everything that we can and we continue to suffer, we must remember that we don't have to suffer. The key here is to see that what is causing us to be upset is our teacher. If we understand this, then it will truly transform our lives. When we learn this lesson, our suffering will go away. Our enemies and our challenges just point to things we need to learn about ourselves. When we learn, our suffering will go away.

I know this may sound too simple, too easy, but it works. When we understand this, embrace it, and put it into practice, we prepare ourselves for positive transformations. This idea is one of the most important tools of living a happy life.

Let me share another story to help explain. When I was in high school, I used to work at a fast-food restaurant. The manager of the restaurant was an obnoxious bear, and I did not care for him at all.

Although he caused a lot of suffering inside me, I didn't want to quit my job. I kept working there, even though I disliked working with this man. I was upset at him very often, and it was hard for me to work there because of him. I knew some people liked him, but I just didn't. Then, one day, I was sitting in a park and I saw an ugly weed that reminded me of my boss. I started to unroll it, for it was wrapped around itself. When I got to the middle of the weed, there was the most beautiful water droplet. I realized then that my boss was like this weed. I might have been struggling with his external behavior, but inside, he was actually a beautiful human being. With my change in attitude, I started to enjoy working with him. It didn't happen overnight, but things started to improve. I did have to set boundaries with him, but my upset feelings didn't last. They started to go away, and I started to feel better about my boss and about my work. This made my life better because when I let go of my upset feelings him and stopped seeing him as a bad person, my suffering went away. My boss was my teacher; he had something to teach me.

Any time we get upset at someone, instead of focusing on that person's behavior, we should ask ourselves, "Hmmm, what's happening inside me that's making me upset? What do I need to learn from this person?" Again, I'm not stating that we shouldn't set boundaries with others or talk to them and try to resolve the issue. Instead, we must remember to examine the upset feelings that we carry inside us when the situation isn't occurring. That's what we want to explore, and that's what we want to learn about ourselves. We say, "I'm upset, but why? What's inside me that I need to change so I won't be upset anymore? These other people, these events, are keeping me from living my fully and richly."

The most wonderful and beautiful thing is that we can change this if we change ourselves. The upset feelings are within us. If we change ourselves, then things will change. These other people or events are our teachers, and we must let them teach us so we can move on and live our life. They have something to offer us, and once we learn the lesson, then we are free.

Chapter Twenty-Eight
When You Get Hit, Relax

If you can master flexibility in life, you will make your life significantly happier. Let me start with a story.

When I was younger, I had finished my undergraduate degree in psychology and was planning to get my master's degree in comparative religion. It was a very challenging time for me because I didn't know quite what I wanted to do with my life. I loved psychology and thought about going into it as my career. But I also loved to learn, especially the religions of the world, and I thought about becoming a college professor. Because I kept changing my mind, I ended up applying to a variety of schools, some later than others. I was accepted into some, put on a waiting list by others, and rejected by a few. In the end, I decided to go to Arizona State University. Though I had thought more highly of some of the other schools I had applied to, I knew ASU was an excellent school, and I was excited to go there.

Once I arrived, I chose my courses and learned I was going to be a TA, or teaching assistant. I was even given my own office with my name on the door. The following Monday, I was going to start teaching and going to school at the same time. It was an exciting time in my life because I finally had settled on what I wanted to do and everything seemed to be in place . . . including my name on a door.

Then on the Thursday before I was to start teaching, I got a call from Princeton. They said, "We know we put you on a waiting list because you applied late, but we now have an opening." Although ASU had a great program, Princeton had been my first choice for studying world religions. You can probably imagine the emotional turmoil I was in at that time. Because I had made a commitment to ASU, I felt I needed to fulfill that commitment. However, I decided to tell my professor what had happened. First, I wanted to see what his thoughts were. Second, if he was understanding of my dilemma and would give me permission to leave ASU, I then needed to see if I could get financial aid at Princeton, because I was one of those many poor students.

When I sat down with my professor, he was incredibly gracious and kind, and he said, "Of course, you can go to Princeton. I know their program well. They have offered you a great opportunity, and we definitely support you in this decision." Excited, I called Princeton, and they were able to give me almost a free ride to go there. So I packed my bags and drove to the East Coast.

What this story is about is that life is impermanent. Life changes regularly, and if we flow well with life, then life will go well for us. If we fight life and its changes, then we're going to suffer. This is an absolute—life is going to change. People we love are going to die, we're going to have to move, we're going to get sick, and so on. Studies have shown that the average person will have six jobs in his or her life, and these may even be jobs they have to get retrained for. If we live in the United States, there is about a 50 percent chance we will get divorced. There are never any guarantees.

Even people that go to school, get a job, stay at that job, and retire, leading a fairly simple, straightforward life will encounter change. They're going to lose their parents or loved ones, may suffer from illnesses, may have children come into their life, and more. Things are going to change for all of us. The only thing permanent in life is its impermanence. If we fight changes (and they are going to occur all along the way of life), then we're definitely not going to be happy campers.

Though it's good to have goals and make plans in life, we definitely have to be flexible. Flexibility allows us to be happy and flow with life instead of fighting it. If we fight life, we're just going to suffer. But if we flow with life, then life goes pretty well. Let me give you another example, using the world of sports this time.

In American football, the receivers on a team take a beating. Their job is to run down the field, catch the ball thrown by the quarterback, run toward the goal, and score a touchdown. It's rarely that simple. What often happens is they run down the field at breakneck speed, they jump up in the air to catch the pass, and just as they catch the ball, a player from the other team hits them as hard as he possibly can and knocks them to the ground. As you can imagine, receivers have a lot of injuries. However, there are professional athletes, like the great receiver Jerry Rice, who play for years and never get injured. When they are asked, "Why haven't you been injured? What's your secret?" they all give the same answer. They say when they get hit, they relax. When they relax, they don't get injured as much or as often or at all.

This is just physics in motion. When you hit something that gives, like a pillow, you don't get hurt because it's very relaxed and flexible. On the other hand, if you hit a steel plate, your hand is probably going to break because the steel plate and your hand are both stiff and inflexible.

People who are drunk and in a car accident sometimes escape injury because the alcohol relaxes them. Unlike sober drivers or passengers who tense up when they are in a crash, the ones under the influence remain flexible. A relaxed body accepts what's coming at it, just as football players avoid injury by relaxing their bodies before impact.

This choice of tension or flexibility and the different results from each apply to life too. When we encounter change, we can respond in one of two ways—get upset with it or flow with it.

Most people choose to become upset. Sometimes, these people turn to something like alcohol to keep them from feeling their response to the change. Of course, this and any addictive vices are our way of not dealing well with change. We don't want to feel it, we want to soften the impact, we want to relax, so we drink or we turn to other substances, or we do other things instead of just feeling the event and going with it.

The other option we have is to relax our minds with meditation. If we relax when things happen and say, "I may not have wanted that to happen, but I'm going to do my best to accept this change because life is a series of changes," then we will be much better off. We will flow with the change and accept that the plans we made have been altered. Even though we don't like that our plans have been changed, we're going to find a way to turn these lemons into lemonade.

For example, perhaps right now you're out of work. You didn't expect to be out of work, but you are. So what can you do? You can, of course, apply for other jobs. But you can also choose to be trained in a new field that you might enjoy even more and end up loving life more. In the end, you'll succeed by accepting the guarantee that change is a part of life and flowing with it.

In dealing with change, we learn that it isn't the change itself that causes our unhappiness; it is our resistance to that change that causes unhappiness. Ultimately, people are as happy as they choose to be. If we want to be happy, we have to choose to be happy. That means that when things happen that we don't expect, then we have to learn to accept them, flow with them, and live our lives well. We are all capable of creating this kind of happiness in response to changes that challenge us. We can choose to live a happy, beautiful life.

Chapter Twenty-Nine
How to Be Happy
When You're Overwhelmed

Over the past several years, my accountant had been encouraging me to incorporate my business. There were a lot of steps involved in doing this, and I hadn't done them yet. Then prior to going on a vacation in Florida, I began to get part of it done; however, there were still a lot of steps I had left to do.

Suddenly, while on that vacation, I woke up with a start at three in the morning. I had been dreaming—I had seen everything I needed to do and everything that could go wrong, and my mind had created a fabulous story of woe. When I woke up, I realized what my mind had done. Up to that point, I had been plugging away at the different aspects of incorporating my business, not worrying about the process, and just doing what I had to do. But my mind had made up this horror story and caused me great stress.. My mind, it seems, wanted to create a story of fear and anxiety.

What I realized was this is how many people live. They create stories about what's happening. But those are just imaginings. What's causing them a lot of stress and worry isn't so much what they're dealing with but, instead, what their minds are creating.

By creating a story of woe, filled with all that could possibly go wrong, my mind had caused me to wake up and feel overwhelmed. I think many people create such stories or stress where they don't have to. My story, like your story, was very real. Every aspect of what my mind had created had some truth to it. There were many steps I needed to take to incorporate, there were things that could go wrong, and the whole process was overwhelming. If I focused on those possible scenarios or on all that needed to be done in a single instance, it would be frightening.

Looking at the whole process and letting it overwhelm us is like opening wide a dam—WHOOSH! The Netherlands with its low-lying land and all its waterways, has some of the world's best experts on building dikes and dams. In order for a dam to work effectively, it has to let the water out little by little. Can you imagine what would happen if all the water was let out at once or if the dam broke? Could you imagine all the damage that it would cause? That's why the water is regulated and let out slowly, so that it doesn't cause any damage.

Our minds are much like a dam. If we watch our minds and we are attentive to them, if we use them for what they are made to be used for—to help keep us safe, to help keep us alive, to experience different sensations in life—then they work pretty well. But our minds can break like a dam and cause a lot of havoc. They focus on everything all at once, and it's extremely overwhelming, creating anxiety and stress for us. For me, this stress woke me up at three o'clock in the morning. For others, they may be living with stress and anxiety for days, months, even years, and it can do harm to our bodies.

So what can we do about this stress our minds create? We can take things one moment at a time, one event at a time.

Here's an example. Let's say we've been diagnosed with cancer. When we get that diagnosis what do we do? Do we let our minds play havoc, thinking about all the negative possibilities—how overwhelming it's going to be, how painful the treatments will be, how unfair life is, and on and on? Or, because we choose to be happy, because we choose to have a good life, do we say, "Okay what can I do? I need to set up appointments with other doctors. I need to determine what choices and treatments I have available to me. I will explore these options one day at a time, one moment at a time, and then make decisions based upon them all." By choosing the latter, we live successfully in life when we are overwhelmed. We take things one moment at a time, one event at a time, and we do that every time, doing it well, and slowly then we will enjoy our journey in life.

Our minds can be on only one thing at a time. If we focus on the beautiful things around us, we will thrive. If we start focusing on the negative things around us, then we are going to suffer and feel overwhelmed. When we focus on what needs to be done right now and that's it, guess what happens? We feel calm and become peaceful. This is one of the reasons I am such a promoter of meditation—it helps us to be in the present and learn to live one moment at a time.

So when we get hit with something like the loss of a job, the death of a family member, our own potential death through a disease like cancer, the best way to handle it is one moment at a time, one thing at a time, and doing that one thing well before moving on to the next thing. Yes, our minds are great at creating stories, but these stories cause us suffering. If we don't want to suffer, if we want to live a happy life, then we need to focus on one thing at a time. When we do this, no matter how overwhelming life can be, it will actually go quite well for us. We can even be happy with cancer or when we lose our job. We can do this simply by being in the present moment.

If we feel overwhelmed by too many things to do, we need to decide which of them we must deal with. Most of the time, we can't do them all right now. Usually, what overwhelms us are things we can deal with in the future. So in this moment, we ask ourselves, "Can I do anything about this right now?" If the answer is no, then we get back into living in the moment, in the here and now.

Our minds trick us by saying, "You've got to find some solution . . . to everything! I'm going to make sure you keep thinking about this, looking at the whole picture and every aspect that can go wrong, so you will find that perfect solution and all will be well." However, this usually just causes us stress and anxiety and no solution at all.

Instead, we can do something else. When we are faced with something overwhelming, we can say, "Do I want to be overwhelmed, or do I want to be happy?" If we want to be happy, then we have to live in the here and now. We deal with things as we need to. We recognize we have a choice—to be happy or to let our minds overwhelm us with the stories it creates.

When these overwhelming events occur, let's choose happiness by living in the moment. It's a very simple approach to being happy; just be here, now, and focus on what needs to be done right now. Enjoy the journey of life, and perhaps you will find, as I have found thousands of times, that when we live this way life goes well. Things just flow.

Chapter Thirty
How the Stories We Create
Add to Our Suffering

Most of us will experience tragedies, both large and small, during our lives. A cherished friend or pet may die, we may become ill, the people who we love may leave us, we may lose our job, and so on. Tragedy strikes so frequently, that we experience suffering on a regular basis throughout our lives. As Buddha so wisely observed, "Life is suffering; suffering is just part of life."

What can we do? Will the ceaseless onslaught of suffering ever end? Is there any hope, or should we just put our heads down and trudge through life?

Yes, there is hope, and this hope lies within each and every one of us. We all have the ability to get through suffering. Either we can let ourselves become mired in our suffering and dwell there for months, years, and even decades, or we can become stronger for having experienced suffering and go on to live beautiful lives.

Let's explore these two reactions to suffering and learn how to make the better, healthier choice.

First, let's look at dwelling in suffering with a personal example. When I was in high school, I fell in love with a girl. I was head-over-heels for her and absolutely convinced I was going to spend the rest of my life with her. There was no one else I wanted to be with. However, our relationship didn't go smoothly. We were together, we broke up, we got back together, we broke up again, and finally, we ended our relationship for good. I can still clearly remember every time she and I broke up. It is entirely normal and even healthy to be upset about a break-up. However, I created an awful story in my mind that just kept going and going and going. I ended up adding so much to my own suffering because I thought things like, "I'll never be happy. She's the only person in the world that can make me happy. I simply must be married to her. I have to live my life with her. My life will be over if I don't spend it with her." It took a while, but finally my suffering did end.

Love can often feel as dramatic as Shakespeare's *Romeo and Juliet* when we are young. It is important to note that the suffering I experienced was far worse than it had to be because of the stories I kept creating in my head. I made the break-up far worse than it needed to be because of my internal monologue, which dwelt upon my feelings of woe, misfortune, and hopelessness. Of course, I needed to grieve and get over the relationship, but it took so much longer because of these stories I created. Yes, suffering happens to all of us. Although it is inevitable that we will experience suffering, if we create negative mental stories as I did, our suffering is going to last so much longer. By reacting like this, we can even transform something that is minor into a huge, awful event.

I see this so often with the people I work with in my practice. For example, one patient was fighting with a sibling over an item left as part of their parents' estate. If I hadn't intervened and helped the two of them come up with a solution, I'm quite sure they would have never spoken to one other again. All that vitriol over a silly little thing! We create stories that often make what's happening in our lives a thousand times worse than it actually is.

We don't have to do this. Staying with suffering is not our only option.

The second way in which we can respond to the suffering we face is to accept and feel our feelings, because it's healthy to allow ourselves to do so, and then to move on. This is the positive way in which to react. A perfect example of this is the typical response of a child. When children get upset, they cry, and then they move on. If we stay stuck in our misery by creating stories in our minds, the cycle of negativity can perpetuate for a very long time. At the very least, we're going to suffer a lot more than we need to. The tragic events we experience in life already cause enough suffering. Our mental commentary about what's happening just makes them worse. If we quiet our minds, if we learn to witness our thoughts and then get back to the here and now, things will be a lot easier. Life will go well, and we will get over our tragedies much more quickly.

I was very close to my mother, and after she passed away, I had an instance where I spontaneously burst out with a gush of tears and sadness, and it felt so good. After this episode, there have been some times that the sadness returns, but mostly when I think of my mother, I remember the good times we had together. I miss her deeply, but mostly I just think of her fondly and remember the wonderful things about her. As I was not terribly old when she died, to lose my mother when I did was quite a shock. She had barely gotten to know her grandchildren. Such a loss could have inspired a lot of negative mental commentary. However, I didn't react so. I realized she was gone and there was nothing I could do about it. I took time to grieve the loss and feel the feelings of missing her, and then I went on with my life. To think of her is truly a pleasant experience now.

The message I am trying to impart here is extremely important: accept the reality, feel the feelings, and move on. If we truly understand it and take it to heart, then our lives will be better.

Most of our suffering is in our heads and springs from the negative stories we create about what's happening. Our suffering is caused not by what is actually happening but by our stories about what's happening. These negative mental stories that we so often create only serve to weigh us down with pain and sadness.

We don't have to be this way. Instead, we can learn how to quiet our minds and be with the present. We must remember that when we are suffering, when we go through hard times, most of the pain we experience stems from the stories we create in our heads. No matter how tragic or awful things may be, let go of the stories. If we don't create these stories, our lives can go very well and we can be happy.

Chapter Thirty-One
Happiness and Ongoing Challenges—
Can They Work Together?

For many of us, when we've reached happiness, we think everything will continue to go well. We think we don't have any more problems and can be happy all the time. But this is only partly true. We will still encounter problems, but we don't have to let them destroy our happiness. When we have the proper tools in place, those bad things that happen don't have to last for more than a few minutes, and then we get back to living.

To be happy even with troubles, we have to acknowledge that problems are still going to happen. If we go on a trip, our flight could be cancelled. When we go to the doctor, he or she could tell us we have a disease. We can be in love with someone, and one of us could fall out of love. Tragedies are part of life.

Once we accept that problems will arise in our lives, we need to react well to them. Instead of what we typically do—spend a lot of energy thinking about our suffering and worrying about these tragedies when they hit—we can deal with what has happened and then live our lives.

Whatever happens isn't a reflection of who we are. It's just a part of life. There is karma, there are consequences, and there are choices that we can make. All the greatest choices on the planet can still lead to problems, no matter how good our decisions were. We can't control the weather. Airlines sometimes cancel flights. Our health is not entirely within our control, even if we exercise and eat well. Think of relationships: we can be the best partner in the world, but we can't guarantee that the other person is going to reciprocate our feelings and behaviors. The other may have issues that come out after we've been together for a while. So, we can't control everything in life, but we can deal with them effectively.

There are several steps we need to take to do well when tragedy hits:

- take any necessary action now
- focus on the present
- eliminate self-criticism
- change our conditioning to bring out positive results..

When something bad happens, we can first pause and say, "Right now, is there anything I need to do to deal with these problems?" Do we need to talk to someone—a doctor, lawyer, insurance company? Do we need to investigate options? Do we need to research online? Then we do what we must or what we can.

And then, or if the answer is no, we can focus on what is happening around us, maybe spending time with friends, listening to beautiful music, going for a walk or reading a book. These are the things that we do to live, and we do them well when we're present. When we are in our thoughts, thinking about our problems, we spend our time worrying. Most people spend most of their time in their heads thinking about things and very little time just living.

When we start doing this, we may go back to our worrying state, so we're going to need some help at first. I recommend using gentleness with changing our behaviors. If we've been doing something for decades, that habit isn't going to change overnight. We can learn a new habit, but it's going to take time. That's why kindness is so important in all this. We have to be kind to ourselves when we keep going back to our worrying states. We need to be aware of our thoughts, to ask ourselves what is happening inside our minds and what can we do instead. Some of us come from harsh conditioning. When we made mistakes, we were attacked for it and spent a lot of time feeling shameful. So this kindness may take some time to learn, and if we surround ourselves with people that apply this philosophy to their lives, it will help us along.

Then, we stop blaming ourselves. Yes, a mistake has happened, and it isn't going to do us any good to be self-critical. Where could that self-criticism come from? It most likely came from our conditioning. We didn't choose our backgrounds, and we can't change our past conditioning. So we don't blame ourselves.

Next, we change our conditioning from now on so we don't repeat those mistakes. We change our conditioning by imagining the behavior comes from our conditioning and by surrounding ourselves with new conditioning. This requires not being self-critical but, rather, learning from mistakes and growing. No matter how many times we mess up, we just keep going forward.

If we change the conditioning, we will change our behavior, eliminating self-criticism. Learning is great, but self-criticism keeps us stuck. We have to be kind to ourselves when we make mistakes. This same attitude applies to others we deal with. Too many of us have a tendency to be cruel and mean towards others, as well as ourselves. Social media makes it too easy to lash out at others when people make mistakes. We all can make mistakes, and it's better to be kind to others and ourselves. Even if it's a huge mistake that lands us in prison, we can still use the opportunity to grow and change, to become a better person.

It is critically important that if we're going to place blame, we put it on the conditioning. If we want to change, we change the conditioning, stop being self-critical, and then move forward.

Once you have something that works for you, whether it's a book, being around a certain person, or listening to my podcasts, you can turn to these things when you hit a dark patch. I have done that throughout my life. When I feel stuck again, I immediately go to my sources that are helpful until I'm back on track. That's one reason I created my podcasts—they can be listened to over and over at almost any place, any time. You can be in worry and just start listening to the podcast or doing whatever works for you. This helps to get your mind back on the present, to switch it off from negative conditioning and back to the present-moment conditioning. That's the way to live.

We can truly have beautiful lives, but we do need to realize that throughout our lives there are going to be mistakes, problems, tragedies that happen. They are not a reflection on ourselves. No matter how enlightened we are, challenges are still going to happen. Instead of obsessing over how we think things should go, we can deal with what we need to address and then flow with life. Mostly we're just living and not self-critical of ourselves for having problems. We learn to live well right now. If we are able to do that, even when bombs strike us, our lives are going to be absolutely beautiful.

Chapter Thirty-Two
The Most Effective Way to
Stay Happy Throughout Our Day

We all aim to be happy throughout our lives. But how can we do it?

Let's start with what blocks our happiness. Why aren't we happy? For most of us, the main reason we're not happy is that we are in our heads too much. We're thinking about things in the past that we wish were different or didn't happen and about things in the future that we want or don't want. Because we're stuck in the past or in the future, we suffer. We create stories. Sometimes our stories are about wishing things were different. For example, "I hate my job. I just want out of my job." Other times, our stories are about trying to figure things out. "Why did my husband have an affair? Why did he cheat on me? What's wrong with me? What's wrong with him?" All day long, our thoughts bombard us. And this is what's keeping us from being happy. When we aren't bombarded by thoughts, when we're just living in the present, we're happy. However, when we have these thoughts, they take us away from our natural state. Our state of happiness is our natural state and happens when our thoughts are non-existent and we're quiet.

The easiest way to prove this is to try meditation. It might be challenging to learn how to meditate, but stick with it, and with time, you'll find it does get easier. When you meditate, when your mind becomes completely quiet and you have no thoughts, you are happy, you are peaceful. Every meditator will tell you this is true. Once you try meditation, you will see that when your mind is still, your natural state is happiness.

Of course, we can't meditate all day long. While meditation is fabulous, it doesn't keep us happy. Meditators who are happy and peaceful when they're meditating can become unhappy the second they stop meditating. All their thoughts can come rushing back, and then they return to where they were before they started meditating.

In a way, meditation is like any distraction. For example, if you just broke up with your boyfriend, you might be very sad. You go to a movie with some friends. If it's a good movie that holds your attention, your sadness will go away during the movie. Your sadness will be pushed to the background and won't be there, so you'll be happy while you're engrossed in the movie. However, the second you walk out of the theater and start thinking about your loss again, your unhappiness quickly returns. That's an example of what happens in meditation: once you stop meditating, the sadness might return.

How do we we maintain this state of happiness? How do we keep our mind still so we are happy throughout the day? Is it even possible?

The great news is YES! It is very possible! Anyone can maintain a state of happiness all day long. And if we can maintain happiness throughout the day, then we can maintain it throughout our lives.

For example, we are driving in our car, but our minds are not on driving; instead, we're thinking about things. We're thinking about all kinds of things. Most of them we've thought about hundreds of times before. But we keep thinking about them. Our worries, our fears, our desires are all bombarding us, we're trying to make predictions. We're trying to fix things that are way out in the future. All we need to do is to focus on right now. So, while we're driving along, we can put on the most beautiful music and listen while we're driving. We can look out and see the scenery go by, different people, the changing weather, and we can enjoy our journey. Sadly, what most of us do while we're driving along is think about stuff, so we miss out on life. We miss out on the beautiful drive and the beautiful scenery that's out there right now.

On our drive, as in our lives, a problem pops up. Someone comes in front of us and cuts us off. Our first reaction is to be upset by that. But we have a choice. We can allow the feelings of that first reaction to keep us upset, or we can instead say, "Well, I'm going to listen to my beautiful music and not let this person affect my day." That's what we can do right now, and we will maintain our happy state. We can't predict if five minutes from now or five years from now we're going to get in an accident and get killed by a crazy driver. And even if we could, in all likelihood, we wouldn't be able to do anything about it. So, right now, we can listen to the music. That's all we need to do: drive and listen to the beautiful music.

The most effective way of maintaining happiness throughout our lives is to focus on the here and now and stay out of the future. We don't know what's going to happen in the future. Yes, we have to make plans and we take appropriate action. But it might take 1 percent of our time to do that. It's the same way with feelings, things that we have to deal with when there are struggles in our life. Those struggles and feelings only take 1 percent to 2 percent of our day to effectively be dealt with.

As a clinical psychologist, sometimes I see that people spend too much time trying to get better, and it doesn't go well for them. In taking too much time, they begin creating too many stories in their heads, and they actually add to their misery. Throughout our day, we all need to be in the present, be focused right here and right now. If all we're focused on what is right here and right now, then we can be quite happy.

So how do we do this? We start being in the present as soon as we get up in the morning. Once we are out of bed, we breathe in deeply and let it out. We just breathe. We don't have to think about the day; our day is planned. Then we say, "Now what do I need to do?" Most likely, for many of us, we have to get ourselves ready for work, for school, or for whatever we have planned for the day.

Perhaps, we meditate at the start of our morning. It really is a great way to begin our day. If we meditate at the start of getting ready for the day, the getting ready for the day will be in the present. We'll get up and have cereal or whatever and eat it one bite at a time, focusing on the taste. It's a newness, a freshness we're experiencing each time. Even if we have had the cereal a hundred times, we can eat it with pure awareness, pure presence of "Wow! What does this taste like?" We put the spoon down while we savor the food. Then we pick up the spoon, take the next bite thinking, "Wow! What does this taste like?" and put the spoon down again, and so on.

With every task in the morning, we do the same thing. When we're brushing our teeth, we are present with just brushing our teeth. When we get dressed, we just get dressed. We focus on how it feels as our clothes to go over our skin, on the colors in the clothing, on the texture of the material. When we're brushing our hair, we feel the brush go through our hair with each stroke.

Then we go on to the next adventure of that day. For me, it's taking the kids to school. Along the way, I often point out the things we see and experience on the way to school. "Did you see that flower? Did you see that bird? Did you see that person?" It helps us to be present throughout the day.

Now this might sound challenging at first. But again, we do it throughout the day. We don't focus on "Can I do this for the rest of my life?" because we have no idea. We're not worried about the future. There are just too many variables that can affect the future. But right now, we can be happy. We can be in happy weather anytime we want to be. But we have to do it now because, once we start trying to make predictions about the future, then good luck because things about the future always change. The ironic thing is that when our minds are focused on the future, when we're stuck in thoughts about what might happen later, we're missing out on now!

To be happy throughout each of our days and ultimately throughout our lives, we focus on what's happening right now. If we do that well, we'll see that life unfolds beautifully, no matter what's going on around us.

Chapter Thirty-Three
Making Time for Happiness

One of the biggest challenges in being happy right now isn't that we don't know how to be happy. It's mostly that we just don't do what we know we should. We don't make the time for happiness, for peace, and for overall joy in our life.

Most of us know if we do focus on the present, it's going to create a good feeling inside us; it's going to cause us to be happy. When we don't worry, when we live in the present moment, when we surround ourselves with people that love us and when we hear loving thoughts towards ourselves in our own mind and we actually work towards keeping our minds quite still so that we're just living in the present moment accepting what is, loving what is, then life goes well. But, what we tend to do, unfortunately, is take on many activities that keep us from happiness and don't allow us to what's good for us.

For example, many of us know what it takes to be physically healthy. We have to go exercise, we have to eat right, and we have to make sure we have proper sleep.

We know what to do, but we simply don't do it. The knowledge is there, but what keeps us from doing it is time. So in order to be happy, we have to make time to be happy. And to do that, we have to get good at saying one little word—no. We have to say no to make room for what is important to us—the specific, such as good health, and overall happiness. If we don't make time to be happy, we're going to be anything but happy, and we don't want that. So, part of being happy is learning to say no to things, and when we get overwhelmed, we just let something go.

For example, over the last year and a half, I took on new book projects, which took quite a bit of time. To do a good job at them and to make sure I still had time for my own peace of mind and happiness, I needed to let something go.

Sometimes things happen to us that are out of our control, and we have to make enough time and space to deal with them. For example, my dog Einstein recently died. He had come to work with me for more than fifteen years, and he had been a great companion and friend. This was a big loss for me, and I needed to make space and time to grieve that. I needed time to heal, so I needed to let other things go, as part of being happy is being loving towards ourselves when we experience tragedy. If we don't make time to be loving in order for us to heal, then we're going to suffer and we're not going to be happy. When there's a loss, when there's a change that is upsetting, most people get busier, or they numb that pain and numbing doesn't heal; numbing just suppresses.

We need to make time for healing, we need to make time for change, and when we get busy, we need to make time for that activity and let other things go so we still have time to be happy. What can get in the way of making time for that are our busy lives, activities, or events. We have to make time when we get busy and let other things go so there is always time for happiness. Happiness takes time, and it comes from the empty space. What I mean is, when we're still, when we're present, when we're just enjoying what is, then our hearts are happy. It's when we are stuck on things and our minds are playing with activities, worries, and fears that we suffer. However, when we silence our minds and we learn to be present, we find that our natural state is happiness, but we have to make time for that.

Any of us can be happy, but we have to make time for it. Even I had to learn to make time for happiness. Over the years, I realized success, achievement, and sacrifice don't work in the long run; they just cause suffering. When we make time to be happy and genuinely fulfilled, then we improve our lives, as well as the lives of people around us. We also then have beautiful experiences that we can share with others, but it takes time. It doesn't mean that we can't achieve anything. But at the same time, during that time I took time for myself and I still meditated, I still spent time in nature, I still spent time with my family, I read, I did things that I knew would work for me and I stayed healthy even though it was a challenging year and a half.

So the key factor here is that sometimes we have to say no to activities or requests, maybe even ones that might be good for others so in the long run we can be good to ourselves. Many moms get caught on this one. They're trying to raise their kids and do a great job, but when their kids are off on their own, the moms are exhausted. Instead, if they spent some time for themselves, they would find a better result for everyone. As the saying goes, "If momma ain't happy, ain't nobody happy." If we are happy, then people around us will feel that, pick up on it, and we create a beautiful world.

Still, we could feel selfish when we do this. Isn't it selfish? There are so many people in the world with so many basic needs. Isn't it selfish when we take time for ourselves? It is selfish, but from giving to ourselves and filling our cups, we can give to others around us. That's the key. We don't give from our emptiness — that's a quick path to burning out. Giving time to ourselves enables us to give to others.

Try this. It might seem selfish, but if we try it for a little bit, try to be nurturing, loving, and giving towards ourselves, then we will see if we are more nurturing, loving, and giving towards others.

Making room for my own happiness is one of the key successes of my life. As a clinical psychologist, I have been helping people for twenty-five years, and I expect to go for another twenty-five years. I think I'll be able to keep it up because I make time for myself, especially as I get older I slow down a bit. I want to continue to help people for the rest of my life, and the way I'm going to do that is to make sure that my cup is full every time I reach out to help others.

Make time for happiness. It does take time, it does take effort, but it has so many rewards that are truly countless.

Chapter Thirty-Four
How to Create a Beautiful Life with Thought

Do we experience life to the fullest or do we suffer through life because of our thoughts and how they affect us?

To help us understand this, we are going to take a brief look at a Korean monk that lived centuries ago and was on his quest for enlightenment. His name is Wonhyo. He is a beautiful person who truly found out what life is all about. He began his quest to live life to the fullest, studying books of enlightenment in Korea. Yet nothing seemed to work for him. He felt he could find better books and teachers in China and set out for that country.

One night on his way, Wonhyo was caught in a gigantic storm and found shelter in a cave. He was extremely tired, worn, and thirsty from his travels. In the dark cave, he found a bowl, and in that bowl there was water. He drank that water, and it tasted wonderful. In the morning when he woke up, he discovered that it wasn't a cave that he was in but an old tomb. Some people had excavated this tomb, and the bowl he had found of was actually a skull. This skull had dirty, black gunk inside it, and because of the rain, it had water in it. When he saw this, he realized the answers he had been looking for! He realized that how he looked at things completely changed their reality. It wasn't the reality that truly mattered, but instead, it was how he looked at things. With that insight, he didn't need to go to China and decided to return to Korea, knowing he had truly found the answers he had been seeking. Wonhyo became one of the greatest teachers in Korean history.

Like Wonhyo travelling in a tempest, perhaps right now we are going through some very difficult things. Maybe our marriage is ending, or we've been diagnosed with a frightening medical issue. Maybe we've lost our job, or we're struggling with aging. Whatever it is, we are like Wonhyo in his storm. We are going through the tempest of life, and we need to find shelter. This shelter can be anything that's happening right now and finding something beautiful in it, in the moment, in the now, in whatever is happening right now.

For example, most of us will experience a parent dying. We can look at it in many different ways. It's like entering Wonhyo's dark cave and finding a bowl of refreshing cool water. Now some may see it as something dark and horrible. But if we look at it in the light of Wonhyo's moment and see it as something refreshing and beautiful, it becomes something positive in a sense. For example, maybe we see that the death of our parent is ending his or her suffering from an illness or debilitating disease, or we see it as our parent's time to be in a paradise where we will someday meet. We can view it as a lesson for us about impermanence; we were blessed with having this parent in our lives, and now we realize we are the parent, the grandparent to our family, and we can focus on that.

There are many ways we can find beautiful, fresh water even in the midst of a storm and even in a dark cave. When we find that beautiful fresh water, even if everyone around us sees it as dirty, dark water in a skull, we will be refreshed by it. We will experience this dark time as something beautiful. We can do this, no matter what is happening in our life. If a relationship ends, if we are diagnosed with something horrible, or if we've been in an accident, there are so many ways in which simply changing the way we think about it and seeing it in a different light completely changes our reality.

The deep truth here is that there is no absolute reality. Whatever we create in our minds will become our experience and our reality. If we create darkness, if we create dark stories, then we will suffer. If we focus on the light and stay present, then we will be refreshed and we will find beauty in anything and everything. If we find fresh water even when it appears to others and perhaps even to ourselves as being dark and work towards changing the way we see things, the suffering will stop and we can find beauty in anything.

Like Wonhyo, we have to realize the power of our thoughts. It's all about how we look at things. If we choose to suffer, we can. If we want to have a good life, if we want to live in the present moment free, ecstatic, and peaceful, we can have that too. But to have that, we must pay attention to what our thoughts are doing. We have to watch them, and when they get dark, it's important that we don't judge them but instead gently work towards changing them. We simply change the focus of the bowl being the skull with dirty water in it to being the bowl with clear water that is so incredibly refreshing. It can be either, but our mind will create whichever reality we let it.

If we put our energy towards seeing our life full of bowls with fresh water available to us at all times, then our lives will become something magical, something beautiful. It's available to any of us, no matter what's going on and no matter how awful things can be right now. All we have to do is work towards changing the way we see things, and then things will change to however we see them.

One person loses his job, and he stays stuck and suffers for the rest of his life; another person loses her job, and she finds something new and exciting to do and enjoys her new career path so much more. One person is in a relationship for many years that ends, and she dives into a deep depression; another person is in a relationship for many years and it ends, but he moves on and finds something better. Maybe he meets someone who is a better match or finds happiness in himself without needing someone to hold onto as he grows in his life or finds another person who is an experience for learning without suffering.

We can always find something beautiful in life as long as we put the effort towards seeing how important our thoughts are, watching our thoughts, and working towards gently changing them.

Like Wonhyo, let's remember to drink the refreshingly clear beautiful water when it's there—and it's always there.

Chapter Thirty-Five
Pause Your Thoughts

When we understand the fundamental element of happiness and live by it, we will be happy. What is it? What is the fundamental key to happiness? Though it may seem very easy, finding the key to happiness can be one of life's most difficult and elusive tasks; yet it is possible.

First, let's explore what causes suffering. Why do we suffer? Some time ago, I worked with a woman who struggled with life. She was a wonderful person, but one of the biggest sources of her unhappiness was her weight. She felt as though she was too heavy and thus unattractive, and she was very self-critical of this fact. She once related to me an episode that had occurred years ago when she and her husband were out on a dinner date. Her husband made a comment about her weight, which wasn't kind. He immediately took it back and apologized profusely for what he had said, but in her head, she kept hearing the hurtful remark over and over. His words stayed in her mind, and unfortunately, she added to this barrage of negativity by repeatedly commenting upon her own weight in very damaging ways. Even though her husband had made the comment only once, ten years prior, his words kept resonating in her brain, and his remark, along with her own negative self-criticism, caused her great suffering.

We did not work on fixing what had happened because her husband truly was sorry for what he had said and the hurtful event had occurred ten years earlier. Instead, I helped her to discover that her suffering was coming from her own thoughts. When she was thinking negative thoughts or making negative comments about herself, she suffered. When I persuaded her to stop thinking these negative thoughts and making these negative comments about herself and just to enjoy life, her suffering was no more.

In over twenty-five years as a clinical psychologist, assisting people whose lives are difficult, I have had clients that are struggling with very challenging situations. Sometimes, a client needs my help immediately. Like many psychologists, from time to time, I get calls from people who feel as if they are going to die and want my help. So what do I do? Do I spend an hour on the phone with them? Do I drive down to my office and meet them there immediately? No. Instead, I do the same thing I have always done. I listen to the person and the situation he or she faces, and then I ask them to go for a walk outside for half an hour to an hour, just spending time outdoors in the fresh air. If after that time, at the end of the walk, the person still feels upset, I say give me a call again. In my twenty-five years, I have never received that second call! I have never had to hospitalize anyone.

Now why does this work? Why does going for a walk, spending time in nature, work? It's because all our suffering comes from our mind. Yes, we have painful experiences, but there's a difference between suffering from the stories in our head and real pain. Pain is a physical or emotional sensation that we feel immediately, and then it passes. Suffering is the story and the dialogue that accompanies the pain, the thoughts we play over and over in our mind: "This is terrible. This hurts. Is this going to last forever? Oh no, oh no, oh no!" That is suffering. Suffering is the mental story that we create. When we stop the negative thoughts and we just *be*, then all is well. Really, all is well. All our suffering stems from the harmful mental stories that we create. Yes, we experience hard times, but those hard times are manageable; challenging and difficult, yes, but manageable. There is no event or situation we can't handle as long as we learn not to react by creating a deleterious inner commentary.

I have known people who have been incarcerated, people dying from cancer, people severely deformed, and people suffering emotionally. Contrary to what one might think, these people were all completely happy because they didn't create a negative mental story about what they were experiencing. They were doing everything in their power to make their situations better, and just as important, they were not allowing the events in their lives to keep them from loving life.

So, the key ingredients to achieving happiness are twofold, yet they are really two faces of the same coin: mental stillness and being present.

When our minds are still, all is well. We don't suffer when we're not creating negative mental stories. We must remember that these harmful stories are in our minds and when we quiet our minds, all our suffering ends.

When we are present, we can always find beauty in something. We can be locked up in prison and yet be mindful of the magnificent rays of the morning sun as they illuminate everything they touch. Listening to our heart beat so gently, so rhythmically, can be beautiful for someone preparing to die and feeling his or her heart beat for the last few times. These experiences can still be beautiful. Yes, these examples may be the exception, but as long as one person on the planet is able to find happiness in such situations, it means it is also a possibility for anyone. Be present, be still. For only then will happiness, instead of being elusive and coming only fleetingly, be our natural state. We will achieve our natural state when our minds are still and living in the here and now without negative mental commentary. If we are present and still, life will be well, and we will experience true happiness.

And if you still do not believe me, I want you to take a challenge. Go outside, preferably where you can find absolute quiet, perhaps a park, a meadow, or a beach. Go to this place and allow yourself to be totally quiet and free from thought for a minute or five or ten minutes. Choose something—a bird, a tree, a flower, or anything else you can be 100 percent attentive to—and listen to this object, watch it, and just be with it. This is all I want you to do for the entire time. Don't analyze the object; just be with it. Your mind is still, and you are being present with the thing you have chosen.

After the exercise is over, reflect upon this time. Were you sad? Did you feel depressed? If you truly were present with your chosen object, you will find that you felt happy and at peace. Yes, this feeling may have lasted only for a short period, but for some people, it's enough to get a sense of "Wow, I can do this!" And trust me, you can!

Keeping our mind still and present is a skill. This is actually a skill we possess as young children, as they do this all day long. However, as we grow up, we forget or suppress this skill. If we learn to employ this skill again and go back to what I call our natural state, then we are happy.

These are the key components of happiness: keeping our mind still and being present. When we learn and put these ideas into practice, we enter the world of happiness.

Chapter Thirty-Six
Finding Hope in Our Hopelessness—
The Strength of Affirmation

We want happiness that permeates our days, our weeks, our years, and our lives, but when we go through challenging times, we can find it difficult to be happy. It's not that we don't believe that it's possible to be happy; it's that what's going on in the moment makes it very challenging to have hope, to be happy, and to believe that, in the end, everything is going to work out for the best.

Whatever our challenge may be—divorce, loss of a home, closing a business, struggling with a major illness, etc.—there is hope in the hopelessness. What can we do during these very challenging times?

Simply repeat the phrase, "all is well."

I've used this over the years when I face a challenging time in life and need to believe there is hope and happiness to come. I steep myself in these simple words that gives me hope. It's a phrase I cling onto when I find myself in hard times. When I'm struggling I don't want something complicated; I want something easy like this that will help me right now. I say "All is well" over and over, and I listen to the words as I say them, whether in my mind or out loud. Although at that moment all may not seem well, just repeatedly hearing that phrase helps and can help a great deal. It can get us through the most challenging times we may ever go through in life.

When we steep ourselves in the phrase "all is well," even though right now we can't tell how things are going to work out to be okay, we get hope. We are inspired to hang in there through challenging times by the power of positive thinking and affirmation. We can, of course, choose to be negative in thought and cry out in pain, and while these things in and of themselves can be helpful in their own ways, we get stuck in the negativity of those thoughts. When we choose to be repetitive in negative thoughts and actions, we get caught up in that negativity and get stuck. Unfortunately, we can stay stuck for a very long time. However, instead, if we choose to believe that there is hope, that with time things will change, and that this too will pass and all will be well again, then just hanging onto that hope can be beautiful and marvelous.

Life isn't permanent. No matter how horrible things are now, things will change. If we hang in there and believe that ultimately all is well, then as we go through this incredibly challenging time, it helps us. It gives us hope, and we move towards healing and happiness and getting well again. This happens because we steep ourselves in the concept, in the hope, in the belief that ultimately "all is well."

When we go through challenging times, sometimes we just want to give up. Sometimes we even want to be allowed to "be in the pain" and believe it's never going to go away. We lose hope. But instead, if we just for this moment listen to and hear that all is well (even if that may seem utterly ridiculous), it can give us hope.

If we allow ourselves to hear "all is well," even though what we are going through is painful, we can get through the next moment. And then we can get through the next moment and then the next and so on. As we continue to listen to our affirmation telling us that all is well, it is more likely that this very challenging time will end and we will win the battle. When we eventually realize we made it through, then we will finally see that all is well, as we affirmed. It's not that we are trying to deny reality, but instead, we are trying to infuse hope into the hopelessness. This hope can make all the difference in the world.

In Viktor Frankl's work, *Man's Search for Meaning*, he talks about living in a Nazi prison camp and those who survived and those who didn't. In many ways, those who did had something to live for— they had hope. Of course, not all who had hope and something to live for survived, but he saw that when people lost hope they didn't last long.

Joe Simpson recounted his ordeal in *Touching the Void* where he fell into a crevasse and lost consciousness. His climbing partner assumed Simpson was dead and, with a storm coming, moved on. Simpson awoke to realize his leg was broken, his friend had left, and he had no hope of climbing out. It was a situation of pure hopelessness. He couldn't climb up, but he asked himself, "Can I move forward and get myself to that next ice opening?" Yes, that he could hope for . . . and he did. He made it to that point, and then he hoped for the next point and then the next; having small glimpses of hope one small step at a time gave him motivation. He was successful because he could crawl those few steps, and he kept dragging himself while he experienced the most horrific pain. Every few steps he would often pass out from the pain; but he'd wake up and say, "I know I can't make it all the way, but I CAN make it to the next rock, I CAN make it to the next creek." He kept doing this for days until he made it to their base camp. Because of those small affirmations, even in the most hopeless of moments, he made it and he lived.

You might think there is no hope left right now with what you're going through. But, perhaps, you can choose to say, "All is well," over and over through the hopelessness in order to get through it all.

I even made a podcast where I calmly repeat the words "all is well" so you can download it and listen to it. You can access it here and keep it with you at all times. You can also utilize your own words and affirmation to seize the moment and conquer those times when all seems hopeless.

If we are going through challenging times, we need to find hope in this hopelessness. We all can do this by positive thinking, affirmations, and simply repeating "all is well" to give ourselves hope, even when it seems like there is none.

Chapter Thirty-Seven
Why We Need Awareness

We're going to explore one of the most essential, crucial ingredients to happiness: awareness. We will examine awareness and the ways in which it is an incredibly powerful tool to help us change.

Have you ever observed people who don't ever reply with retaliation when someone hurts them with words or actions? I once knew someone who would do this, and it was so refreshing that I asked him how he managed to do it. "Are you just a very patient person who never says anything mean? Do mean thoughts never pop into your head?" I asked. The person chuckled and explained to me that, no, mean thoughts would indeed come into his head from time to time. However, instead of spewing them out, he would pause and reflect, just for a moment, thinking, "If I say these unkind words, what impact would they have on the other person?" If he thought the words would indeed be hurtful and mean, then he wouldn't say them. I learned something that day that changed my life in a very beautiful way. I learned that, yes, I can feel my feelings, but if I pause and think before speaking, I can be a nicer person. Although it is not always easy, I strive to be a nice person, and so I found this lesson to be wonderful and incredibly valuable.

The key ingredient that helped me to change my behavior was awareness. Prior to this discovery, I wasn't aware that I was speaking without considering the impact of my words. I acted a certain way, thinking it was appropriate, and it was the way everyone behaved. In reality, mean words definitely pop into everyone's head occasionally, but some people take the time to think before speaking them. Awareness is so crucial to being happy because we can change only if we are aware of what we are doing, of how our actions affect ourselves and others, and of the need for change. If we're not aware of something, we definitely can't change it! Being aware is truly a very effective way to bring about change.

Let me share another example. I work with many men who are successful and feel driven to provide well for their families. They think, "If I work extremely hard and make a lot of money, I can retire early, my family will be well off financially, and all will be well." However, what they're not aware of, and I do mean this, is that the ends don't justify the means. These men think that if they work hard, even though they're never home and their wives and kids never see them, that in the end, years later, when they are home all the time, everything will be great, and it will all turn out for the best. What I teach them is that this won't work; this is not realistic. I say, "Go home sometimes! Be with your family! You can still be successful, although it may take longer. Most important, however, you'll have a family that is intact. You'll have a wife and kids who love you, who enjoy you, and who know you. If you do this, life will be a lot better, a lot less stressful, and a lot happier." With this new awareness, these men do begin to change their lives.

We all can do the same thing in our own lives. It's crucial not to be judgmental of ourselves but, instead, to look at ourselves and ask, "What's happening right now? How is my life going?" If there are any aspects of our lives that aren't going so well, then we can use awareness to bring about change. Again, we are not judging, just looking. We must speak to the other people in our lives, asking, "How is it going? How are we doing? How is our life going overall?" Perhaps you could even reread these inspirational messages, learning how to achieve happiness. With our newfound awareness, we can all bring about change in our lives.

To change our lives and achieve happiness, we need to know what's going on. We often lead our lives in ignorance—not stupidity, but ignorance. The difference between the two is that when we are stupid, we aren't smart, but when we are ignorant, we just don't know better. It's best not to be judgmental with ourselves and instead to say, "Oh, I just didn't know that." With these new tools that we've gained, we can begin to change our lives for the better in a healthy, productive way that works. Again, awareness is the critical key of change. When we have awareness, when we understand what's happening, we can look at our lives and then initiate change.

Part of being aware is saying, "I am going to take a hard, honest look at my life." We can't numb ourselves. We can't come home every night and have three or four glasses of wine because our lives aren't going well. This type of behavior is not going to help us very much.

We need to be aware and ask, "Honestly, how are things going?" If things are not going well, then we use this tool of awareness to say, "How can we change it for the better?" When we do this, we are practicing non-critical awareness. We are just looking and examining, really exploring and talking with other people in order to become fully aware of who we are and what we do.

When something in our life is not working, this awareness can bring about change. Only then, will we realize, "I come home and have three or four drinks to deal with my life and then I end up yelling at my family. Instead, I'm going to come home and go for a half-mile walk to unwind and see if this helps, to see if things go better." And of course, things are going to be better because we've become aware of our former actions, we've found a new way to deal with our tensions and stress, and we're going to be approaching our family in a whole new, positive way. We're going to get rid of that stress, and with our newfound awareness, we're going to be a happier, healthier person, and everyone in our life will benefit from that.

We must remember that awareness isn't criticizing, but instead, it is neutrally observing. It lets us wake up to what's really happening. With this new view of the situation, we can start bringing about change. If we aren't aware that we are doing certain things, then we can't change them.

Awareness is a beautiful way to bring about change in our lives. It's a non-criticizing, powerful, and amazing tool that we can utilize to bring about positive change, and with this change, happiness.

Chapter Thirty-Eight
Relationships and Being a Great Partner

We all have relationships—we get married, raise children, have friendships, or interact with people at work. They're part of being human. So it's important for us to learn how to be happy in relationships.

How can we find happiness while we're in good relationships? We can find the answer in being happy when we're single. You might be wondering how being single has anything to do with being in a successful relationship with others, but it does.

When we were in high school, there were different groups of students, based on members' interests. There were the jocks, the academics, the ones in the band, and so on. They were just different groups, and like most people, we tended to hang out with like-minded people. But there were also youths who often didn't know about themselves, and it's almost as if they fell through the cracks and ended up hanging with others feeling lost. They made poor choices and didn't do well in life. We're not here to judge those people who were struggling—we're here to love them—but we are here to learn. In life, when we're not doing well, we tend to attract people that also aren't doing well.

When two people who aren't doing well individually get together, they just don't do well together, and things go downhill from there. It's a sad situation, and we all know people like that. Again, we may be in relationships like that right now. We're not feeling very good about ourselves, and we realize the person we are with isn't doing well either. We end up creating a lot of negative energy. So being in a good relationship always begins with being good to ourselves when we're in a healthy, happy, peaceful place. That's what we're going to attract and be attracted to—people who contribute positively to our lives, instead of people who are crazy or make poor decisions.

Our friends and partner impact us, and we impact them. When we are in a good place, we can be attracted to people who are also in good places. When we have a family member that we don't get along with or we are forced to work with someone on a regular basis that we clash with, being in a good place can be helpful for them. At least, we can set good boundaries with them and not join them when they make poor choices. If they want to go out and get drunk every day after work, we will not. We can still love them; we just won't join them.

So, it's critical in life that we are in a good emotional state—happy, loving, caring, etc.—if we want to find a good partner, a good mate, a good friend. If we want to have healthy relationships, we have to be healthy, and we can determine how healthy we are by the types of relationships we have. Instead of asking ourselves how we are doing, we can simply look around and see whom we are spending our time with; how well they are indicates how well we're doing.

If we are doing well—eating well, exercising, spending time in nature, doing things that are good for us—then we're not going to want to join other people in dysfunctional activities. It's actually very beautiful if we think about it because if we are doing good things for ourselves, taking excellent care of ourselves, we're going to be in the situation where other people are doing the same.

Even though we're well past high school, we still hang out with people that have similar interests and backgrounds. If we start making our self-care a priority, we're going to want to be with people who do the same thing. The key factor in all of it is that we need to be in a good place if we're going to attract good people. How can we be amazing and beautiful people, loving life, living well? What if we are ready to be in a relationship with someone else? In the beginning, we need to be focused not on them but on our self. How are we doing? What are we doing to take care of ourselves? We need to make sure our mindset is in the right place. It's all about eating, exercising, and all the different things we do for self-care.

Everything matters, and when we make ourselves a priority, if we take care of ourselves and make good choices, then whether or not we have great relationships, we are going to be doing well because the main person we turn to throughout our life is ourselves. If we learn to take good care of ourselves, make good choices, and make sure we're doing well, then when we experience a shortage of good friends, we're going to be doing okay. But, we're also going to be doing things to attract other friends because we're going to be putting ourselves in a situation that's good for us. Other people are going to be there, and with time, we're going to meet some amazing people when we do things that are good for ourselves.

Most of my closest friends I met when I was focused on my passions. When we do things that are good for ourselves, other people are there, too, and we're going to meet them, and life's going to go well. But we always have to bring the focus back to ourselves. What's happening in our mind? What are we thinking about all day long? Are they beautiful, peaceful, loving, thoughts? Or are they harsh and critical thoughts? We can fool the world, but we can't fool ourselves. If we don't like ourselves, we're not going to be attracted to people who like us. We're going to be attracted to people that don't like us, and this can create a bad situation for ourselves. But, if we learn to love who we are, love our life and live it well, then we are going to experience that. Whether or not we find our soul mate, journey with people that may come and may go, go through a period of time of solitude in each situation because we have to learn to love ourselves, we're going to be doing well. So, again in relationships the key factor is how am I doing? Where is my heart at? What's happening inside me? A lot of it is being aware and looking within ourselves, watching ourselves and asking ourselves how we are doing. What is your internal dialogue like all day long? It's like a conversation we're having with ourselves. What is it? Is it good? Is it positive? It is harsh? Is it negative? It matters whatever it is.

We want to have periods throughout the day where we are still, where we can just be quiet, but we have to learn to watch what's going on inside us. If we don't, we may be attracted to people that are negative towards us if we are negative to ourselves. We are going to attract what we feel about ourselves. Someone else can't make us happy. Happiness is an inside job! If we are happy and loving towards ourselves, then we're going to attract like-minded people that are happy, love us, and love themselves.

In order to be in a healthy loving relationship, we start with ourselves and ask, "How am I doing? Am I in a good place?"

If we want to be in a great relationship, we're going to work on being a great partner. And the way we attract a great partner is by learning to love ourselves, being peaceful, and being happy inside. We can all do it no matter what background we have. The focus has to be on ourselves instead of searching for someone to fix us.

Chapter Thirty-Nine
Relationships: Finding a Great Partner

Finding a great partner involves two parts: being a good mate yourself and looking for someone who is as much like you as possible.

These two parts interact and affect each other. For example, the second part relates to the adage, "Birds of a feather flock together." This is the correct adage because we don't want to make decisions based on thinking that opposites attract. Yes, they do attract, but in the long run, they don't do very well. So we are looking for someone who is as much like us as possible. But, we first need to look at ourselves: if we are a great partner who is loving, kind, supportive, listening, taking good care of ourselves, being healthy, being happy, and so on, that is what we are going to attract. However, if we are dysfunctional, struggling, and having a hard time then that's also what we're going to attract. So yes, it is so important to find someone like us, but we also need to be like someone we want to find. Let's look at these ideas more closely.

We need to be the kind of partner we want. We need to be in a place that's healthy and take care of ourselves. If we don't do that, then we will attract someone who is unhealthy and isn't taking care of himself or herself. Now this isn't an absolute guarantee, but the way to avoid dysfunctional relationships is by being that healthy person because if we are we will not be attracted to dysfunction. We may date it, but we won't date it for very long. It will quickly end. This could also apply to friendships and family. If we are healthy, we won't put up with dysfunction. It just won't be very attractive to us, and when it occurs, we will just set up boundaries. The boundaries could include not allowing others to continue to hurt us, ending some situations, and so on. In dating, we will quickly end dysfunctional situations because even if dysfunctional behavior isn't initially directed at us, eventually it probably will be.

We each function within a metaphorical behavior bubble, which has very clear rules that we follow. It indicates how we treat ourselves, as well as others. So, for example, if we are harsh on ourselves when we make mistakes, then we're going to be harsh on others. We sometimes let people into our bubbles. We get married, and our spouse enters the bubble. We have children, and they enter our bubble. When others do, we start treating them the way we treat ourselves. Let's say a couple is dating, and the man is very romantic. He gives his girlfriend flowers, writes her poetry, and says a lot of endearing things to her. They get married, and then everything changes. What happened is that it isn't the love that lasted. He was treating her like he wanted to be treated. He didn't want flowers, he didn't want poetry, so he didn't verses to her anymore. He still cared for her but in the same way that he cared for himself. So when we're dating, we have to watch out for this.

How people treat themselves and other people indicates how they might treat us. How are they treating their friends, their family, and most important, how are they treating themselves? When they make a mistake, do they angrily punish themselves? What is their self-talk like? It may not be easy to pick up on that, but if we observe, if we take our time, the truth will unfurl, and we'll begin to see how they treat themselves. Then we'll begin to see how they interact with our world. When someone hurts them, do they get really angry or upset? When they go through a tragedy, how do they treat themselves? When we have an argument with them, how do we interact during that argument? This isn't that hard to figure it out; it just takes time. So let's give ourselves time; that's probably one of the most important things we can do. The longer we take to get to know someone before we decide to commit a life to this person, the better we feel.

How others treat us does matter. We're not going to marry or get into a serious relationship with another if the person is treating us poorly. But most important, we have to look at how they treat themselves. If they're treating themselves in a harsh way, sooner or later that's going to be directed at us. We have to be honest. So often I see people expect they can change their partners' bad behavior. It is far better to assume that whatever is happening is going to stay that way or perhaps even become worse. If they drink too many beers, if they yell at people too often, if they're stuck in their job and seem depressed, that's probably going to be their way for the rest of their lives. No matter how much we love them, we can't change them very much. I make a living trying to help people change themselves because I stay neutral while they decide and work to change. But in a relationship with someone with bad habits, any motivation to change his or her behavior has to come from that person and not from someone else. And often, people stay the same.

Look at what relationship you have and ask yourself, "Do I want to spend my life with this, or am I hoping to change my partner?" If you do, then drop that. It may not be the perfect person for you if you want your partner to be different.

If we can live with our other's differences, if we can live with his or her fur balls and the things we struggle with, then great. If we can't, we need to decide whether to stay in this relationship or not.

One other common mistake I see is that while people are looking for the right partner, they hang onto an old relationship. Lots of people do this. I used to do a show called the *Holistic Success Show*, and I had the number one relationship blogger in the world on my show. He said the very same thing—what most men do is stay in old relationships that are going nowhere while they're hoping to find another one. What he and I encourage is to end the relationship and be single so you can find someone you are looking for without sabotaging new relationships because you're hanging onto the old one. You need to let it go and work on being single. It's healthy to be single. It's good for you to be by yourself and enjoy that solitude. When we're single and are able to be in that state, we're not going to feel panicky or make bad choices. We need to be happy with ourselves before we find our partner. If we can't be alone, then we probably won't be a very good partner.

Part two in finding the great partnerships and friendships that last a lifetime involves looking for others who are as similar to us as possible. How do we find these birds of like feather? I suggest four ways:

1. Do what you do with passion and seek others doing the same.
2. Use friends to expand your relationship circle.
3. Be open to using the Internet . . . and use it.
4. Trust that all will work out.

Number one is to do what we do, do it passionately, get out doing it, and then look for people that are doing it too. Passion in what we do attracts others, and by engaging in what we love to do, we attract others who are similar to us. But we have to be out doing it and making ourselves available and known, if only in a little way. By doing what we enjoy, we are authentic, presenting a true picture of ourselves.

Different types of activities attract different personalities. A Star Trek convention brings a certain type of people different from a meditation retreat. We need to enjoy our passions and do them, and then look around and be friendly.

People need encouragement. Women, pay attention. A nice guy is not going to be aggressive and make the first move without an indication he should make that move. If he's a nice guy, he is going to wait for you to give a little smile or some hint that you are interested; otherwise he'll respect that boundary that you have made. Being cold works with setting up walls, but if you want to attract someone who is kind and gentle, you need to give some indication you are interested.

This is the beauty of taking our time by watching the person we are maybe interested in and seeing how he or she acts. We will observe what he or she is like and then decide if this is the type of person we want to spend time with and get to know better. If not, we walk away. If yes, we give a little hand and wait to see if the person brings us anything back and proceed from there. It's a gentle dance that we both have to participate in, and women, nice men need some encouragement, so give them some.

The second way we can meet people is through our friends and other people we know. We have to let them know we're interested because our friends and family want to help us. Going on a blind date can be scary, but meeting someone through friends doesn't have to be a blind date. They can have us over and invite the other person too so we can see if we're a good match. Letting our friends and loved ones play matchmaker is a good way of our finding a mate because they know us so well. But we have to put the word out that we are looking.

The third tip is using the Internet. I know some do not like this idea, but I urge you to consider it because the Internet has become a very effective way of finding mates. When you do use it, put out as much information about yourself as possible and then look for people who have a lot of information about themselves, too. We're looking for someone like us. But if we say only, "I'm pretty" or "I'm handsome," there's nothing for people to know about us beyond the superficial level. If our profiles are detailed and so are those of our potential mates, we can get a better idea if we would be a good match. We're looking for depth and for likeness in interests, and by making our profiles as detailed as possible we make it possible for the other to find us.

When we find someone who looks compatible from an online description, then we need to ask many questions before we meet in person. Although the Internet allows relationships to develop very fast, it's going to be better for us if we take our time in getting to know another through an online connection. We need to take time to make sure that the other person is being truthful because people lie, and the Internet makes it easy to do so.

The key factor with Internet dating is finding out as much information about others as possible and also sharing with them our likes, dislikes, and hopes for the future. Most dating sites let you use filters to pick out what you want or don't want in the other person, which also increases your chances of finding the right mate. But if we're secretive, hide information, or lie, then later it could bring problems or obstacles to the relationship. For instance, if you start dating a person but don't mention you want kids in the future, you might be afraid the person won't continue to date you if he or she discovers you want children. We need to put out all our information so we can end an unsuitable relationship quickly.

It can be a lot of work to find someone through the Internet, but it is also encouraging because it works for so many people. It does take time to find the right fit. If you want to find the perfect dress for a dance, you will probably have to go to several stores. It's the same way with finding a mate. In the same way you might take a dress off the rack, look at it, try it on, and study it while it's on you, do the same with meeting people on the Internet. If one person isn't going to work out, move onto the next one. Asking questions will help you discover a lot of information you need to know before you meet in person. If you find you have a lot in common, proceed. The Internet can be a very effective tool if we use it well.

The fourth point is trusting in God or the Universe to help us find what we're looking for. When we are in a good place, taking care of ourselves, then God, or the Universe, help us find what we are looking for. We don't have to be alone in this. It's almost as if, when we are in a good place and comfortable being alone, all of a sudden everything synchronizes to help us move in the direction of finding our soul mate, finding that person we can spend our life with. But, we have to trust. We can increase that trust by being comfortable with being single until we find our soul mates. We have to like our time alone as we are looking for people to journey with us in life. With this balance, God will help us find the mate and friendships that are best for us.

To recap, remember these two things when looking for a good mate. First, be a good mate yourself. Second, find someone who is as much like you as possible. When you do this, you will find happiness and a happy relationship.

Chapter Forty
Relationships: Keeping a Great Partner

In order to maintain a great relationship, we need to work on them. They are a lot like exercise.

If you want to be in great shape, you have to work out regularly. If you want to keep a great relationship, you have to work at it. If you get in shape and then rest on your laurels without doing any more exercise, you will get out of shape. If you work on a relationship, get it to a comfortable level, and then relax without attending to it anymore, the relationship has the potential to get out of shape. Both parties must work on it. You don't know what the other person will do, so it's important to do your part. You say, "All I can do is my part. I can't do my partner's part, but I can do mine."

How do we make sure we are doing everything in our power to work on the relationship and keep it healthy? A large part of this is through connections. In relationships, it's often through romance.

A few years ago, I took a course called Organizational Psychology. It's about giving psychological help to companies. I distinctly remember my professor saying the companies either grow or they die. They have to be doing one or the other; otherwise they stay the same. Relationships are lot like that. We need to nourish them, we need to work on them, we need to spend time with them. There are many things we can do, but we need to make the relationship a priority.

Sometimes, we might take friendships or marriages for granted. It's a lot like physical health. We can be in great physical shape and then think we don't have to continue going to the gym. We all know what's going to happen with that. This is no different from couples keeping their relationships in shape. When they don't work on their relationship, they will begin to have problems. So no matter what's going on—if we have children, if we are moving, if we are starting a new career or going back to school— our relationships still require time and effort. I know it takes two partners to make a relationship work, but all we can do is do our part. We need to ask ourselves,

"Am I the best partner I can be?" And if the answer is yes, then it's going to be a little easier to move forward if we have to.

What are we doing today about our relationship? What are we doing this week? What are we doing this year to make sure this relationship is getting our time and effort because if it isn't, it's not going to do as well. It's often why relationships falter: one of the two people in the relationship stops making it a priority and focuses on other things, maybe other people, other activities, other interests, and then the relationship begins to die. So let's frighten our brains that we have to work on the relationship and we can't take it for granted. It takes effort, ongoing effort until the day the relationship dies. We have to put effort into relationships to maintain them.

So what can we do to maintain that healthy relationship? What specifically can we do to make relationships work? We need to do three things:

1. Make the relationship a priority.
2. Be kind to our partner or friend.
3. Engage in common activities together.

First, we make the relationship our priority by devoting time to it. Obviously to exercise and work out, we have to make time to work out. To keep a successful relationship, we have to make time for that relationship. If we don't regularly connect with our partner or friend, that relationship is going to begin to falter. We ask ourselves how much time we are spending with our partners. Are we going on dates with them? Are we texting them? Are we calling them? Are we stopping and having lunch with them? It's very important to make sure we have time with our partners, with our friends, because otherwise, like a flower unattended, the relationship will begin to wilt and eventually die.

Relationships take time. In working with couples and helping them build a healthy relationship, I focus first on their having time together, including going on dates. Even when people have been married for decades, they still need to go on dates, particularly if they have young kids. Most often, a difficult time of marriage is when people have young kids at home and then they just don't make time for each other. So when I work with couples, I make sure they're going on dates regularly, at first once a week if they have to get a babysitter. They need to make sure they can say, "This is something we have to look forward to." With time, I get them to take a weekend away and then, with a little planning, to go away for a week. It is very healthy for us when we are in a relationship to get away for several hours or even days, spending time with just our partner.

I know it's hard to do, particularly when there are children. But it is a very healthy choice because children benefit when their parents are doing well; children don't want parents that are arguing or fighting. They want love in the family as much as the parents do.

The second important part in maintaining a healthy relationship is being kind and gentle with each other. Couples may spend time together, but if they fight and argue, the relationship is not going to thrive. It can be difficult to stay in an intimate relationship or friendship if too many harsh things have happened.

When I work with couples, I set rules. It's okay to talk about things, but once a partner is becoming intense, it's important to take a break. But couples get afraid that if they take a break they won't talk about the topic again, so they keep going. To address this concern and still lessen the tension, I suggest they do something to reduce stress, such as a walk to get away from the situation, and then agree on a time when they can talk about it again, such as in an hour or the next day. We can't continue the conversation in the heat of the battle. Once emotions get intense, a break is critical to maintaining a healthy relationship, and we will continue the conversation after we get calm. Too many couples just try to keep going through, thinking they're finding a solution. They think they will feel better and can resolve the issue when strong feelings are flying, but they don't realize that when we're upset it's a horrible time to keep going and try to resolve an issue. There are just too many emotions, and often we can't think logically.

It's like trying to talk to someone who is drunk. We don't try to have a meaningful conversation with a drunk person, and when a person is angry, he or she often can't think clearly. So if we give the one dealing with intense feelings space and take some space for ourselves and say, "Let's talk about this tomorrow" or "Let's take a break and get back together in hour," we will feel better.

Sometimes it is good to find a third party like a therapist to help us through problems, but it's important to stay calm and loving, no matter what. That is a great way to maintain a healthy relationship because when we're calm, we're going to listen to the other person. We're not going to say derogatory things, and we're more likely going to work through the issues that we have to work through.

Issues or problems can come up, and they can be a bit challenging to work through. We may disagree with our partners, so what should we do in such a case? Sometimes we have to make decisions where we disagree. What do we do when we both agree to disagree? What are our options? When we have to make a decision, we have three choices as a couple:

1. We can agree.
2. We can compromise.
3. We can take turns.

I use this all the time in therapy, and it's a very effective way to navigate decisions when we have disagreements. For example, we're going to go on a vacation this year. The first option is to agree. We can both agree that this year we'll go to Hawaii for a vacation. Wouldn't that be great? Yup, that is great. This is an easy situation; we all know how to make decisions when we agree.

But let's say, for example, I want to go to Hawaii but my partner wants to go to New York City. What are we to do then? We can take the second option and compromise. Perhaps, we say, "Let's not go to New York or Hawaii this year; instead let's go to Santa Fe."

If we disagree, we could also take the third option and take turns. We could say, "We haven't been to Hawaii for a long time, so let's go to Hawaii this year, and then next year, let's go to New York City." If we agree to take turns, we have to honor them; we can't try to talk our partner out of it next year. Let's be respectful to the other person and to ourselves, and respect means if we say something we stick to our word. We agree to it.

It's very simple to make decisions if we agree. When we disagree, we have to either compromise or take turns because if we don't, resentment is going to take hold. Fairness is a beautiful way to have a relationship work well. When we both feel that we are being fair, we both take something away from it, and then we feel good about our relationship. But if we aren't trying to be fair and instead are focused on winning, on putting the person down, and on getting our way, resentment builds, and with time, resentment can turn into a loss of care to our partner, and we don't want that.

When we began our relationship, we likely had things we liked to do together. Over time, we may have grown so far apart that we no longer have common interests. If so, we need to try new things and find activities to do together, because intimate relationships, like friendships, are built on having similarities. We need to have things in common that we both enjoy doing because, if spend time together in happy pursuits, we strengthen our relationship. We'll have happiness and a fond feeling for our partner, which makes our relationship healthy.

I had a friend who worked hard on developing his career, and he did not have much in common with his wife anymore, so every week they took a day off together, and they just found things to do. They tried different things until they found what they enjoyed doing together.

Because we are committed to our relationship, including friendship, we do need to make that effort and find things we can do together that we both enjoy. This may involve a compromise. If only one of us loves camping, maybe we could stay in a log cabin and we both could enjoy nature with a little more comfort than camping in a tent. If one of us doesn't like sports events, maybe we could join a low-key sports group, such as co-ed volleyball, and have fun, make new friends, and spend time together. This involves a give-and-take attitude and the openness to try new things.

There are numerous activities we can do with our partner if we want to maintain the relationship. We have to have some things in common—we don't have to do everything together; it's fine to have different interests. Some activities we do with our friends, and others we do with our partner. We have to have some things that we do just with our partner. These things are ours and make us say, "Wow, that was great to do together." Like eating healthy food, engaging in fun activities with our partner gives vitality to the relationship. If we infuse our relationship with love and the memories of having good things to do together, it puts smiles on our faces that are going to make us like our partner more and enjoy our relationship so much more.

To recap, we can do three things to maintain a great relationship. First, we have to make the relationship a priority and to devote time to it and our partner or friend. Second, we need to be kind, romantic, and loving in a relationship. Third, we develop and engage in activities we like to do together so we look forward to spending time with our partner or with friends.

By following these three steps, you can develop a very loving relationship with your partner. If you're unhappy in your current relationship, ask your partner, "Are we doing these three things? Are we spending time together, being loving, and creating fun memories together based on things we both enjoy?" If not, figure out how to do that because relationships are worth it.

All we can do is our part; we can't make our partner do his or her part. But if we do what we need to do, then at least we're going to feel good about ourselves. No matter what happens, we will be able to say, "I'm capable of being a good partner. Maybe it won't be with you, but I'm capable of being a great partner."

Sometimes our partners do change in a way that challenges the relationship. Sometimes they get addictions or go with someone else; sometimes they have disorders that affect them in the long run. So be it. All we can do is focus on our being a great partner. We take care of ourselves and are a great partner so, no matter what happens, we can look in the mirror and say, 'I like me because I was a great partner in this relationship." We're going to be okay because we took care of ourselves; that's the ultimate focus. The second focus is having our partners participate with us in making this a great relationship. We do our part, and that is going to make us feel good and happy.

Relationships take work, but it's worth it for a life partner or awesome friend. And, we will attract great people if we are great partners and friends, allowing us to be in wonderful and fulfilling relationships.

Chapter Forty-One
Dealing with Loss

How do we deal with loss, whether death or break-up, of those we love? We may think we're going to have our relationship until the very end, but with rare exception, even if the partnership remains intact, one of us is going to die first, and the other will have to deal with the loss of his or her partner and friend. It's important to know how to deal well with the loss of a partner as we navigate the course of life and relationships.

Let's begin by looking at why relationships end. The simplest explanation is that one of the partners dies. "Partner" may be our best friend, a parent, a dear work associate, or our spouse. Other times, we experience a loss when our partner decides to end the relationship. The person might be unhappy or has changed or just doesn't want to be in the relationship anymore. It can happen to any relationship—marriages, friendships, business partnership; even parents can sever a family tie. We will all go through a loss of some relationship. We may be the one ending the relationship, or we may be the one left behind. In either case, it's going to happen to all of us at some stage.

So, how do we handle this loss well? How do we deal with the end of a relationship, a partnership, a great love? Let's first consider the situation where we are the ones to leave. When we want to end the relationship, how do we do it? First, we have to acknowledge the other person most likely will feel hurt. One of the ways to be happy in life is to cause as little suffering to others as possible. Yes, sometimes we have to set up boundaries to protect ourselves— perhaps the person we're with became an alcoholic, is cheating, has become abusive, or whatever. But we still need to end the relationship in a loving way. We're going to cause the other suffering, but we don't want to inflict pain on them if we can help it. No matter what the other's response is, if we do it in a loving way, it makes a positive difference in the outcome. Often, people at the end of a relationship become very cruel and vicious; they attack their partner, and that is only going to cause harm to that other person.

And when we hurt other people, if we are a hurtful person, we are not going to be happy ourselves.

If we have been thorough and feel as if we've done everything in our power to keep this relationship alive but now it's time for us to end it, we should do it in a very loving way. Even if our partner responds cruelly, attacking us or being vicious, we need to maintain our loving stand and not attack back. Boundaries are okay, such as, "You can't cross this line, or I'm gonna leave."

So let's not enter the world of cruelty. Let's not enter the world of meanness, no matter what the other has done to us. Let's choose to be gracious. This can mean simply that we don't talk to our partner anymore after stating the relationship is over. Usually, ending it involves more than that—explaining what happened and how we've done everything we feel was possible to make the relationship work. Maybe our partner won't agree. Regardless, it's always important to end a relationship lovingly because that person matters and how we act matters in how we view ourselves. When the dust settles and the other leaves, we will think more about what we said than what the other did.

For example, over the years, I've worked with many people that have been in a domestic violence relationship. Although usually one person is doing physical harm to the other and the other leaves, often the other goes back to the abusive partner. Why do those who are abused go back? Sometimes I see that when violent incidents occurred, the abusive partner had responded to hurtful words that the other person was saying. So when the dust settles, the abused one thinks, "He [or she] probably wouldn't have responded that way if I hadn't said that," and there's some truth to that. That's why in a relationship it is always so critical to focus on ourselves and our behavior, which is all we can control, because if we do need to end it then we will end it well and kindly.

Sometimes, we end relationships way too prematurely. We don't want to look back and say, "I wonder if I should have tried harder." So often we leave not because we worked hard but because we want something else. It's important particularly when there are children involved that we work on keeping the relationships as best as we can. Help in doing this can come from many places—professionals, friends that love us and support us, books, workshops, etc. Always focusing on being a great partner means also seeing how our partners respond to that. If they see our changes, then we can be in love with them or at least maintain a great friendship.

If, after doing everything in our power to make the relationship work well and it ultimately doesn't, then we end graciously. We're not going to send a mean text. We're not going to talk badly about our former partner to other people. We're not going to find the most vicious lawyer and create lies so that we win in court. Instead, we're going to be loving and kind. Yes, we will set boundaries so the other cannot hurt us, but we're not going to respond back in kind when the other is mean. You'll never find the person who was vicious to another in a relationship that is ultimately happy. Look at the people that you know that have ended relationships viciously. Even if they were the victim of cruelty, they won't be happy. Relationships end. Sometimes we end them, and if we do, we do so in a loving and kind way.

Relationships can also end through death or our partner breaking up with us. So how do we deal with that? We all know we can't control life or death. The relationship ending due to death can be horrible, even though we had nothing to do with it. We might have been with someone for years, and they died in a car crash or were diagnosed with cancer that left them with only six months to live. I've had a situation like that happen to me, and it's extremely challenging. The other way a relationship ends is when the other person says it's over. It can also be very hard to face that rejection. Not only is the person gone, but he or she has also chosen to leave us. Whether it's the loss of a friend, family member, or romantic partner, we're all going to face some form of such a loss.

What can we do? How do we deal with a relationship we thought was permanent ended, not by us but by outside forces—by death or by our partner?

To get over the loss of a relationship, we must acknowledge that anything we have is impermanent. Everything we have is a gift, not something we have to have or need to have; it's something we would like to have, a preference. If we think, "I won't be happy unless I have this person in my life," that way of thinking is going to cause us to suffer even if we have the most amazing relationship. Sooner or later, the relationship will change, either through breaking up, death, or the typical ups and downs. The attachment to this relationship can cause us to suffer. When we realize how important it is not to get attached to the relationship, we actually love even better because then every day is a special gift. We will be saddened by losing the relationship, but we will realize that it was part of life and we are not guaranteed anything at all.

Of course, we will do anything in our power to work on our relationships, but ultimately they can and do change. When that change happens, we need to feel and express the sadness over it, and then we need to live. Life is filled with joys and activities that we love, and yet we are suffering because we feel we have to have that one relationship.

Think of it this way: pretend we have a garden filled with wonderful flowers. We love roses, but for some reason, the roses all died in our garden. Wouldn't it be silly to grieve over the loss of the roses if we still have other beautiful flowers? Our life is like that garden. We have many beautiful people in our lives, but sometimes one leaves us. Of course, we will be sad over the loss of that dear friend or partner, but we still need to enjoy all the beautiful things God has given us. When we learn how to let go and love all the gifts we do have, we're going to do so much better.

Part of what we need to do in dealing with loss is to recognize the difference between sadness and depression. When we're sad, we grieve, and then we feel better. When we're depressed, we grieve but after the tears, we don't feel better. We might even feel worse because our minds are creating stories, such as "I'm never going to be happy again. Why did this happen to me? What's wrong?" Those thoughts keep us stuck. A healthy expression is "I'm going to miss that person. It's very sad she left, but I'm going to be okay. I am going to let myself grieve, and then I'll move on."

Let me use an example of how this works. Years ago, I had a cat that I just adored. He was a sweetheart, and we had a very special bond. One day I came home, and he was very sick. I discovered he had feline leukemia, and he died shortly after his diagnosis. When he was alive, we had a song we liked, and every time it came on, I would pick him up and swing him around the room, dancing with him. I don't know if he liked it or not, but I sure did. After he died, whenever I heard that song, I would cry. I would cry during most of the song, and it felt good afterwards. I would think, "Oh I feel so much better." I allowed myself the tears. It took about two years not to feel my eyes fill with tears when I heard that song. That's healthy grieving. I didn't spend all my time grieving, but I did allow myself moments to grieve. Of course, if our mate has died, we're going to spend more time grieving. But still, it should be limited. If we're grieving all day and we don't find ourselves feeling better, then we're struggling with depression, not sadness. Sadness heals; depression keeps us stuck. So, we need to realize that as we go through the grieving process there are no guarantees. Relationships end, but life is full of so many things we can enjoy. When we do enjoy what life offers us, life's going to go better, we're going to feel better, and we're going to realize that this is the best way to live.

When we love well, we can realize that God gave us a gift and when it is taken away, we can be sad but our life will go on. Of course, it's going to take time to heal, so we have to be gentle with ourselves. Perhaps projects we've been working on can be put on hold, or we can take a break from activities. We need to take time to heal; otherwise, we will suffer. Part of the human process is being kind to ourselves, perhaps getting involved in a support group, just doing things that are gentle and nice towards ourselves because we are in the grieving process.

Avoiding the necessary grieving, like becoming super busy or turning to alcohol, does not heal. Those activities just suppress our feelings, and sooner or later that grief will come rushing back if we don't take the time to heal it. We must also heal in moderation. We're not going to spend all our time healing—that's probably going to become depression. If we take a bit of time every day, give ourselves time to think about what we've lost, and feel sadness or anger, that can help us. We can feel anger, but we express it in appropriate ways. We don't lash out at the other person. It's healthier to write in our journal.

It's not always easy, but we need to be kind to the other person when he or she leaves us. Behaving with kindness is the best thing we can do to heal. We need to take the time to heal, and we're going to do that if we give the other person space. We can't constantly reach out to the other person or abuse the person. A lot of the time, when people are hurt, they want to hurt the other person back. This will keep us stuck. We want to learn, grow, and move on in a positive way.

It can be helpful to imagine not having the person we love with us anymore. Perhaps it's imagining a spouse asking for a divorce, a child dying, a best friend not wanting to be in our lives anymore. It's not just that we're grieving; we're also making sure our hearts see the people as gifts that are impermanent and will change. If our hearts can say, "Of course I don't want that to happen, but if it does, I will be okay," then we will be okay if it happens.

Also, we'll find that we will love better because we see people as gifts, not possessions. If we see that God has given them to us for us to enjoy now, not that they are guaranteed to be in our lives forever, we will love better. The only person we're guaranteed to travel life with is ourselves, so we love those who join us in our journey but recognize that sometimes they will not be around anymore. However, we can still love deeply, and if we allow ourselves to heal, then when something ends, we can move on and do a lot better in new relationships as well as in life.

Let's make sure we're taking good care of ourselves, our hearts are in the right place, and we're loving ourselves and loving others, learning to be happy in the here and now.

Chapter Forty-Two
Eat Your Mental Fruits and Veggies to Be Happy

Organic fruits and vegetables are good for us, especially when they are eaten raw. This is what I eat, and I have lots of energy. However, it hasn't always been this way. When I was growing up, my dad used to make us his favorite potatoes on special occasions. He would slice up a bunch of raw potatoes and cook them in a vat of very unhealthy oil. We would eat them, dripping with that oil. It tasted great when I was a kid but, as I learned later, it certainly wasn't very good for me.

Over the years, I've learned to eat better. Now my body's become so used to eating healthy foods that when I do eat something that's very rich, it tends to make my stomach upset. My favorite morning juice is a blend of organic fruit and vegetables. Some friends who've tried it don't think it tastes very good, but they're just not used to it as I am.

So what does a diet of fruits and vegetables have to do with happiness? Our minds are just like our bodies. If we feed them good material—healthy, positive, loving images and thoughts—we do well. If we don't feed our minds these things, then we don't do well.

For example, as a clinical psychologist, I often work with children from divorced families. Sometimes when these kids' fathers see them on weekends, and the fathers unthinkingly take the kids to movies that are clearly inappropriate for children. When I see these kids in therapy during the week, the first thing they want to share with me is the movie their dad took them to see. They sometimes talk about the movie with a sense of excitement, but I can clearly tell that they feel a need to get it off their chest about how it scared them or made them feel upset because they really were too young for it. As adults, we're not any different in our reactions to negative influences in our lives. It's just that we've become numb to the effects of negativity.

Imagine for a moment that, when we're born, we're like a five-thousand-gallon water tank, and inside our tank, the water is crystal-clear. At one end of the tank, there's a tube feeding water in, and at the other end, there's a tube that allows water out. Our minds are just that simple. Things come into us all day long, and they go out of us all day long. As time goes on, the water in our tank starts getting muddied and dirty. So, when new junk comes in, we don't even notice it; we only notice the dirt coming in when the tank is clean and crystal-clear. Then as we get older and the tank becomes darker and dirtier, when a batch of new negativity comes in, we can't even recognize it as junk. It's amazing how we can get so used to such unhappiness and think it's normal and, even worse, we sometimes pursue it.

One night many years ago, I was driving home very late, and I passed a casino. It was a Tuesday or Wednesday night around one in the morning, and there were so many cars in the parking lot that I just couldn't believe it. I'm not a gambler, but I decided to stop in for a little bit to see what was going on. Hundreds and hundreds of people were there. I looked at all the slot machines and the gaming tables, and then I looked at the expressions on the peoples' faces. I didn't see one person who was happy and having a good time. They all seemed very depressed, upset, and angry . . . far, far from being happy, and yet here they were on a work night, spending their free time and hard-earned money doing something that seemed to be causing them to be unhappy. My guess is that their water tanks were very dark and murky. They couldn't even tell that what they were doing was causing them unhappiness. We can get like that if we're not careful. I know this was an extreme example, but even in our regular lives, I think we have to be careful and ask ourselves, "What am I feeding my soul and mind all day long?"

I think everyone would agree that doing harmful things or being exposed to harmful things is very unhealthy for us. Extreme situations, like a rape or having to fight in a war, have negative effects on us; we all understand that. But what about negative images and shows on TV? What about negative conversations? What about negative things we read? What about what we watch on the news? Do these things affect us?

In my practice, I've counseled several women who have husbands that don't come to therapy. They stay at home, and sometimes these husbands get in a dark state of mind spending a lot of time watching the news. Instead of simply learning about the events of the day, they're spending hours and hours listening to and watching it, hearing the talking heads analyze it, getting fully involved in it, and becoming depressed. I suggest to the wives that their husbands stop spending so much time watching the news. After they do stop, the wives report to me that their husbands have started to feel better. These are men who are supposed to be strong and brave, yet they are being negatively affected just by watching the news.

Here's another example. If a really angry teenage male tells you what kind of music he listens to, I'll bet it isn't something like Mozart or love songs or any music styles that are peaceful and happy. It's almost always music that is harsh and upsetting. Not that everyone who listens to such music is angry, but rarely will you find an angry teenage male who doesn't listen to that kind of music. Now, we can argue which came first, the anger or the music, but clearly the two are correlated. It's logical that what we watch on TV, what we think about in our heads all day long, what we talk to other people about, what we listen to on the radio, what music we listen to, everything that comes into us affects us. *Everything.*

So if we're striving for happiness, then first, we need to pay attention to what we're thinking all day long, and second, we have to look at what we are exposing ourselves to. Once we notice, if the influences are negative or our reactions and behavior are negative, then we make changes. If we begin to make even small changes at first, we will experience more happiness in our lives. A little improvement today can add up to a huge improvement in the long run.

If we want to change our eating habits because we eat terribly, we can start just by having a salad with our meals and maybe some fruit with our breakfast each day. It doesn't completely change our diet, but it does make improvements in it, and if we continue to do it, then over time, we'll become a healthy eater.

We do the same thing with changing the negative influences on our minds. The first thing we have to agree upon is that whatever we listen to, whatever we watch, whatever conversations we take with us in our heads do matter. Next, we need to ask ourselves, "How is this affecting me?" If it is affecting us negatively, then we have to start making changes. The bottom line is that everything matters. So we have to pay attention to what we are thinking, what we are watching on TV, what we are listening to, what our conversations are like because it matters.

This isn't about feeling guilty; this is about being happy. If we want to be happy, then we have to have happy thoughts in our head and expose ourselves to positive, loving things, rather than negative, harsh things. Those are the healthy fruits and vegetables for our minds. So we begin by paying attention to what we're thinking all day long and what we're exposing ourselves to. Then if they are negative thoughts and influences, we can start making some small changes, and in time, those small changes can add up bigger positive changes.

Remember the water tank. At one end, we're going to start feeding crystal-clear water in. At first, even as we begin to make changes, what will be coming out the other end will still be the same old gunk. But with time, because the gunk is going out of the tank, the water inside will start to become crystal-clear again. Then happiness will be something that we are, instead of something we are pursuing.

Chapter Forty-Three
Identifying with the "No-Self"

Do you know one of the main reasons we suffer? The answer I give may surprise you. We suffer because we identify with ourselves.

Let's start from the beginning to explain this. Go to a park where there are many children of all ages and watch them. The younger kids you'll find will be playing, doing very silly goofy things, and they are completely oblivious to what other kids or even adults are thinking about them. Then observe the older children. They're not being so silly and usually conforming to someone's standards of proper behavior. As children get older, they begin to say, "What does Mom think about me? What do my friends think about what I'm doing right now? What do classmates think about what I'm wearing? What do others think about what I'm saying?"

And with time, they start to identify with themselves, saying, "This is who I am, and I am this way because of the way people treat me. I must be a cute person because people tell me I'm cute. I must be intelligent because people say I am smart. I must be really funny because people laugh at my jokes."

We begin to identify with what other people think about us and what we call ourselves. Our interactions with other people influence how we see ourselves, and from them, we develop a sense of self. But this self that comes from others causes us suffering because it may not match who we really are. We may not like the identity that has developed around us; we may not like what we give to ourselves and what other people give to us; we may not like it when people disapprove of us—and it is very challenging to go through life without someone disapproving of us at some point. Even if we try hard to follow the rules and do right, someone out there is going to disapprove of us. The world might love us, but someone will still disapprove of us.

Every day the tabloids are full of examples of people who are incredibly accomplished but in rehab centers for drug or alcohol addictions. How does this happen? It's because, even though they've accomplished so much, they still don't feel happy inside; they still struggle with discontent. The world might love them, but if they don't love themselves, it's not going to work.

We give way too much credit to that part of us we call the self. But how real is that self? How truly permanent is the thing we call the self? We're always changing . . . our taste in music, in food, even in people. Our personality changes, and so does much else about us, yet we always hang onto the rigid sense of self: this is who I am. But really, it's a case of "this is who I am *right now*." We do change, so why do we hang on so tightly to that sense of self? When we do that, we suffer because we really care what other people think about us and how we have defined ourselves. If people like the self that we are identifying with today, we feel great. But tomorrow if someone disapproves of our sense of self with which we're identifying, then we can feel horrible. We're putting ourselves on an emotional roller coaster: it goes up and down. Up and down, we go with our emotions based on what we think about ourselves or what other people think about us.

If we no longer identify with the sense of self that isn't that real anyway, we can just be free to be like a young child—we can be free of what other people think or feel, we can be free of what we think, and we can just live our lives. Then we're going to find happiness because we're not going to be so concerned about what other people think or about getting their approval. Doing things just because we want to do them generates happiness in all of us, but we do have to let go of that self.

When we were younger, our defined self had a small grip on us, but as we got older, it started to paralyze us. This can be challenging to change because we have been conditioned for years to care about what others think.

We can reverse the influence others' opinions have on us bit by bit, and the more we reverse it, the more happiness we're going to find. We do that by having small pockets of not looking at or listening to other people's opinions. We begin to change with small steps. It can be as simple as wearing an outfit that we normally wouldn't wear just because we want to. Now, we have to be a little careful here because if we're not confident about what we're doing, we're going to look at other people and see if they approve or disapprove of us. If we give them our power, we are going to lose that sense of spontaneity. We have to surround ourselves with people that are kind, loving, and accepting and stop paying attention to what other people think. When people want to share their opinion with us, we have to be careful that it's very beautiful and positive, and if it isn't, say, "Well, that's okay; I don't really want to hear it." People want to comment on a behavior, but if we work towards letting it go unless it's beautiful and loving, we'll do better.

So if we can live one moment at a time, we'll free ourselves like a young child and we'll discover life can be beautiful. The small changes add up and make a difference. Perhaps the next car that we buy will be the one that we want, not based on what other people will think; perhaps the next outfit we get will be what we want and not based on what other people think; perhaps the next home we live in will be based on what we want and not what other people think. If we live spontaneously, as we go along, we ask ourselves, "Hmm, what sounds like fun right now? If it doesn't hurt anyone, why don't I just do that?" Why don't we just run in the rain? Why don't we just go for a swim? Why don't we just sing a song loudly in the shower? If we're not hurting others and we're not hurting ourselves, then perhaps we can live a more spontaneous life and let go of that self and just be.

We can be who we are without being so concerned of what others think of us and what we think of ourselves. We can see the children playing in the park, and we'll be like them, living freely and happily without concern about others' opinions. Instead of having attachments to who we are, we will *just be.*

Chapter Forty-Four
What's Our Identity?

How can awareness be the cornerstone of who we are? After all, we have families, experiences, schooling, memories . . . don't all these together create, make, and define us as who we are?'

All of these things definitely play a role in who we think we are right now, but the key phrase to remember is "who we *think* we are." The truth is that who we think we are is in constant flux, changing all the time.

For a moment, let's close our eyes and recall who we were exactly four days, three hours, and ten minutes ago. Can any of us remember? Clearly our memories are not exact—they change, they transform, we forget things, we have new memories that replace some of the old ones, or we talk to someone else who may see the same thing differently than we do, and then we change it in our minds. We change our memories! Therefore, our memories of who we are change constantly.

For example, let's say that when we were in elementary school, we were very shy and hesitant to make new friends. But when we got into high school, we joined the drama club, and we became more actively involved with our fellow students and even enjoyed interacting with other people. When we went on to college, we took on an entirely different persona, a different identity. Perhaps we became the party animal, or instead, we became the academic scholar. We wear many different hats throughout our lives.

When we go to family, high school, or college reunions, we may notice that, yes, there are characteristics in all of us that remain the same over the years, but there are also many things that change. Now we look different, we have more or different interests, we have new friends, we may be married and be a parent, and we act very differently than we did in high school or college or some phase of our youth. We change as we grow older. If we are constantly changing, how can we possibly say we are "that" when we are not "that" later and we weren't "that" before?

Let me use the example of a typical teenager to illustrate this point. A typical teenager wants to stay out late to be with his friends and doesn't care that his parents are upset and worried about him. He doesn't give much thought to the feelings of others or even to his own safety. He just wants to have a good time. Then, later in life, when the same teenager becomes a parent, he's now cautious and concerned, as his parents were. Like a metamorphosis, the once a wild and crazy teenager has now become an anxious and overly cautious parent.

Since we frequently change, who are we really? When we reach retirement, again we change. We may become a recluse, we may become an alcoholic, we may become a person who loves to travel in a motor home and explore the world, we may move into a monastery, et cetera. There are so many different ways we change. We may become a grandparent or a great-grandparent. Which identity are we? If we keep changing, we're really none of them.

Then, who are we?

We are awareness, and our experience can be the proof of it. Let's try this together. Let's think back to one of our earliest memories of a significant event, perhaps when we started school or when we were a young child at home on our birthday. One of my earliest memories is when I was about two or three years old. I was visiting my grandparents on their farm in Iowa, and there had been a huge snowstorm. There were these absolutely massive snowdrifts that I would climb up to the top of and slide down. I was having a blast! When I think about this memory, I can see it as if it is fresh, happening again right now. I can witness it and be aware of my feelings without labeling them or without labeling myself, and they feel exactly the same way as I experience things today.

Many years later when I was in Sequoia National Park with my children for a holiday, we experienced a huge snowstorm that piled about six feet of new snow on the ground. I went sledding down the hills of snow with my children, and again, it was a blast. Though I am, of course, a very different person than I was at two or three years old, my witnessing or my awareness of what I was experiencing in the snow on that day many, many years ago was the same. I was aware of what was happening in both instances. I was awareness.

So who are we then? We are awareness. We are aware of our experiences. When we're around two or three years old, we begin to label things. We see that we like this and we don't like that, and between those two poles, we create our personality. We have likes and dislikes, and we take on labels, even though they change over time. What doesn't change is our awareness of what's happening. We are aware; that's where we start.

Perhaps a better way to understand this concept is to say, "We are right here, right now. *We are.* All our memories are in the now. All of our future ideas are in the now. Everything is right now." The only thing that is right now permanently, that always has been and always will be, is our awareness. We aren't being us when we take on labels. They're not really who we are because those labels can change; they are transitory. But what does stay the same is our awareness, and if we reside there, we begin to relax. We become happier.

When we don't reside in the now, in awareness, and we instead identify with those labels, then we fear something. This causes us suffering. Even desire can cause suffering. Even if our desire is great and we have it met, it's going to pass and it's going to change and that change, that fear of losing something, that longing for something, can cause us suffering. Remember, all the ideas of who we are, are in our head; they're concepts, and they keep us from just enjoying life. We enjoy the snowdrifts of life a lot more when we don't label things and we just play in the snow, whether we're one hundred years old or two years old.

When we identify with our awareness instead of identifying with our labels, we take a much more childlike approach to life, and this is good. To us, then, life is new, it's fresh, and it's exciting. When we label something, we miss out on it because we don't truly see it anymore. But when we keep our minds quiet and we can just be, the awareness of life as it is, without all those labels, the beautiful adventure of life, can be tremendous. It can be amazing as long as we stop labeling things so much and just flow with life.

Here is one simple technique to stay in awareness, to stay in the witnessing state. Whatever we are doing, whenever our minds start thinking, we are missing out on life. So when we do that, we must remember just to get back to living. Let's experience what's before us: let's look around, check in with life, and let our thoughts become quieter and quieter. Let's allow our egos just to relax, and we can say, "Everything is going to turn out okay. I'll just enjoy this journey of life." By being in the present moment, life will proceed a whole lot better.

Chapter Forty-Five
Cutting the Puppet Strings of Praise and Blame

We're all familiar with puppets with strings attached to their arms and legs. When someone pulls the strings, the puppets move in different directions. The puppets do the bidding of the one pulling the strings.

Unfortunately, we're not very different from these puppets. Let me explain. We may walk into a restaurant, and the waitress may comment on how we look, perhaps saying how nice our outfit looks, and this may make us feel like a million dollars. We may feel as if everything is going well and we are on top of the world. Our self-esteem puppet string has been pulled up by the waitress's comment. However, later that same day, we may run into an old friend, and he or she may comment on how tired and exhausted we look. Our self-esteem puppet string may be pulled down by our friend's comment, and we may feel ashamed, upset, and sad about our life. It's amazing how other people, by what they say about us, pull our puppet strings and cause our emotions to go up or down. Clearly, we are often greatly affected by what people say to us and what they think about us.

Let me give you a few examples of this kind of behavior. When I was in high school, our teacher in a speech class asked us, "Why do students work so hard to get letters on their jackets?" He was referring to varsity letter patches, earned from excelling in sports, band, academics, or some other such activity, which were sewed on a jacket or sweater. Everyone in the class gave the teacher different answers as to why students worked so hard to "letter." But the bottom line was that people did it so others would think highly of them. It was a way of saying, "I've made it! I'm successful! You should think highly of me. I do, don't you?"

We can all laugh at that now that we're adults and say, "Well, that's silly." But think about it . . . does it change that much in our life as we grow up?

When I was working on my PhD, I was talking to other PhD students who said, once they received their doctorate, the main thing they were looking forward to was being called Doctor So-and-So. Again, we may laugh at that, but give it some thought. Why do we care so much about what people think about us? We do a lot to make sure others think highly of us. We buy certain cars, live in certain neighborhoods, wear certain clothes, hang out with certain people, name drop, and on and on it can go.

The reverse is true, too. We are affected negatively by what people think about us. We may fall into a pit of dire desperation because people think we've failed. Maybe we've lost our home, we're in bankruptcy, or we may even think of suicide because others seem to think of us as failures. It's amazing how those childhood puppet strings never get cut at any age and how strong they can be.

However, if we want to be happy, we have to cut those puppet strings. We have to stop caring about whether people approve or disapprove of us. It's not that we're going to become callous and uncaring. It's just that, in order to be happy, we have to let go of the strings that hold us up to praise or blame. We have to let them both go. It's easy to let go of blame when people are attacking, when they're saying something mean. It's easy to say, "I'm going to ignore that." But we also have to ignore and not hold onto the praise that can come our way. That can be hard to do. There can be a subtlety at work here, because we often are guilty of looking for or soliciting other people's praise. I'm not suggesting we should reject praise or ignore criticism. It's just that we can't let our lives be controlled by it. We need to let them go. We need to see we have a choice—we can have others' praise and blame, or we can be happy. If we want happiness, then we release being controlled by what others think of us.

We're doing what we want to do because we want to do it. We wear what we wear because we want to wear it. We're driving what we drive because we want to drive it. All the things we do, we do because we want to do them and not because people will be impressed by us or not think lowly of us. We're just doing it to do it.

Many people fall into this trap with their profession, choosing it or staying in it because of the prestige, rather than working in a less desirable job that more closely matches their interest and passion. It doesn't matter what we do. But we will be happier doing things because we want to do them and not because of what other people will think of us. If we do things because of what other people will think of us, then we're puppets, and that makes life hard. It makes happiness for us more elusive, more unobtainable, and puts it in the hands of others.

If we want to be happy, we have to cut those puppet strings. Those puppet strings are going to be there if we listen to and are affected by what others think about us. It's not that we're trying to be rude. It's just that to be happy, we must be child-like and who we are because of the way we are.

Anyone can do this, even those who seem most attached to following what others think. For example, I heard a story about a man who was a suit-and-tie type of businessman and very successful. But he harbored a criticism in his mind about other people and the way they dressed, particularly if men didn't wear a business suit as he did. However, because he was a wise person, he realized he needed to change this thought process. So for one month, he dressed very flamboyantly. But at the end of that month, he found he liked his new style so much that he continued to dress that way for the rest of his life.

What can we do to cut our puppet strings? First, we have to be aware of what the puppet strings are, who is holding them, and what's affecting us. With that awareness, the second step is to begin to stop buying into them; stop listening to those holding the strings. The best way to do this is not to solicit comments from other people, and when comments come anyway, just discount them, essentially ignore them. It's nice to get praise, and it can be hurtful to get blame. But, if we don't give so much credence to the criticisms and praises of others, and instead, just flow with life and live in the present moment doing what we feel like doing right now, we can cut the puppet strings. As long as what we do doesn't hurt another person, then life is going to go pretty well. It's a matter of getting out of our heads, living in the present moment, and enjoying the journey of life by doing what seems good right now. We just ignore the criticism, accept praise without letting it affect us, and realize neither does us much good. They can even be harmful; even praise can be harmful.

So by not paying attention to praise or criticism and, instead, living in the present moment and choosing exactly what we want to do simply because it sounds like fun and something we want to do right now, we will make our life more free. Our life will no longer be controlled by the puppet strings, and we will have a beautiful life, an adventuresome life, and a happy life.

Chapter Forty-Six
Kindness: The Currency of Change

We've all made mistakes, hurt someone, or hurt ourselves and then wished we could have done differently. But how do we bring out the most effective way of no longer doing that? How can we create change to stop hurting ourselves and others?'

First, we have to acknowledge that we're self-critical. When we make a mistake, oh wow, do the devils come out! Then they stick us so many times in so many different ways that we can't get the mistake out of our minds. But we're so used to our self-criticism that we almost don't realize what we're saying.

For example, when we put on those few extra pounds, we get on the soapbox of self-criticism. We look in the mirror and call ourselves names, we feel our body in a very self-critical way, we notice what other people are looking at and think, "They must think I'm a flat blub." Unfortunately, this self-criticism works. It makes sure that we're going to stay heavy because all day long we are hearing the negative comments in our heads. Thoughts are incredibly powerful, so we hear these strong messages that we're fat, fat, fat. So at the end of the day, are we ready to resist that dessert? Not likely because throughout the day, our thoughts have been critical of ourselves, of our ability to resist temptation, and of our weight, zapping motivation.

Second, we must deal with our mistake with kind thoughts. The most powerful thoughts are our own because these are the ones that we hear all day long. If we want to bring about change, we have to be kind towards ourselves, and the only way we're going to be kind to ourselves is through awareness. If we're not even aware of what we are doing because we're so used to being self-critical or we think it doesn't matter, then we're going to get stuck and stay there for the rest of our lives. We don't like to hurt ourselves or others, and we don't want to live miserable lives. We can begin to make some changes, first, by acknowledging that thoughts do matter. They are not neutral. If we're self-critical towards ourselves or others, such thoughts will impact us. If we want change, we have to have kind thoughts.

Think about it this way. Say we have a choice between two teachers, both very knowledgeable in their field but each with a different method of teaching. Now, let's say we want to learn how to do yoga. Teacher Number One criticizes us every time we don't get a pose right. Teacher Number Two uses kindness, love, compassion, and gentleness. Which teacher would we prefer? Of course, we would choose the latter because that one will be more enjoyable and we will learn faster. Our minds are the same. If we want to learn to change, we will have a more enjoyable time and learn faster if we use kindness on ourselves.

Let's use the weight analogy again. Suppose we've put on a few pounds and someone made a negative comment about it. It was very hurtful, and perhaps we felt angry and upset about it. But the truth is we're going to be more critical of ourselves and our weight gain than the other person could ever be. Once we start understanding that criticism, especially what comes from ourselves, isn't going to motivate us to create change, we can replace the criticism with kindness and start making the change.

Many people struggle with change because they're focused on the negative part of their behavior, instead of bringing about positive change in their lives. If we change what we focus on and start using love and kindness to create change, it will make a real difference. Think of alcoholism. Until relatively recently, alcoholics didn't have much hope of ever breaking their addiction. But then about a hundred years ago, two wonderful men started an organization called Alcoholic Anonymous. When alcoholics trying to break their addiction relapse, instead of beating themselves up with criticism, they can go to an AA meeting and learn positive steps to take. They learn they have a disease that doesn't have to end their life, and they receive support in making changes. The main thing that changes here is that kindness replaces self-critical remarks heard all day long.

We are gentle with ourselves and learn from our mistakes. We can ask, "What can I learn from this?" We can say that a thousand times because it's not self-critical. When we focus on what we did wrong, we're probably going to repeat the mistake. But if we focus on how we can do better next time and without self-criticism, we can learn from it. This is going to enable us to do a whole lot better in creating change.

I see this work so effectively in my practice. People come to me and share their horrible stories, things that were done to them and, more important, what they did to other people. With gentleness and kindness, I help them understand that if their conditioning had been different, those things would not have happened. So if we change their conditioning, we can have a behavioral change. That kindness, that act of loving them and hearing their horrible stories, is caring for them and helping them get better. We all can get better with kindness.

When we mess up, we have to be kind to ourselves. We have to realize that two things caused us to be this way. One is our genetics; the other is our conditioning. We may not be able to change our genetics very much, but we can change the conditioning, and one of the most important ways we can do this is to start using kindness instead of criticism. I think people often resist this because they're afraid that if they use kindness it's going to give them a license to continue doing the behavior they want to change. They think if they're kind, then they'll continue doing it. But this isn't the case. When we are aware of how our behavior affects others and ourselves, we realize self-criticism isn't bringing about anything good. With awareness, we can say that we will change with kindness. We have to be kind towards others and we have to be kind towards ourselves.

It's not that we shouldn't set boundaries. Of course we need them to protect us from others who hurt us. But we can still be kind. We can also set boundaries with ourselves. For instance, if we battle with drinking or food addiction, we can stay away from those substances or situations that cause us to drink or overeat. We can also surround ourselves with people who help us make good choices.

We can change, and kindness is the way to go about creating that change. Criticism might work, but we're not going to find happiness with it. If we want to be happy, we use kindness as a tool to create change. Then we can work towards finding happiness in our lives. If we're happy, we can find ways to help others also be happy in their lives. It then becomes a beautiful circle. Kindness works. It creates beautiful, positive change.

And that change with kindness begins with awareness. We can't change something if we're not aware that we're doing it. So, we watch our thoughts and see what they're like. We don't judge them; we just look at them. If we notice that our lives are permeated by negative thoughts towards others or ourselves, we just acknowledge that and then start changing them. We avoid self-criticism, which is not effective for making positive change. Instead, when we observe a negative thought, we ask what we can learn from the mistake it's addressing and then move forward. If we mess up again, we repeat the process—see what we can learn from it and once again move forward. It's about reconditioning the brain. If we believe this, we will do it and become good at it.

With awareness and kindness, anyone can change. We're worth it. We can be happy through kindness. Kindness works.

Chapter Forty-Seven
Why We Need to Be Kind to Others

Recently when I was driving, I pulled over at a local gas station to fill up my tank. I went inside the station and gave the gentleman behind the counter twenty dollars before going out to pump my gas. When I had finished, I noticed that I had been erroneously given thirty dollars worth of gas instead of twenty. I immediately went back inside and handed the man another ten dollars, explaining the situation. He looked astonished and thanked me profusely. As I drove away, I thought about what had occurred. I asked myself why the gas station attendant was so surprised that I had walked back in and given him that extra ten dollars. And I asked myself, "Why did I do that?" My experience at the gas station on that day inspired this article about the benefits of being kind, honest, and loving to others.

I am not going to explore the typical rationalities for my behavior, the ones you have undoubtedly heard many times over, such as, "You ought to behave justly because God is looking over your shoulder" or "You ought to behave honorably because this is what your parents taught you." The truth of the matter is I didn't act for any such reason. Indeed, my thought process was much simpler.

What would I want to happen if our roles were reversed, if I were working at that gas station? As a gas station attendant, if I mistakenly gave a customer ten dollars of gas for free, I might get into trouble with my boss over the discrepancy. I could even lose my job! If I did lose my job from my oversight, I might not be able to get another one in this sluggish economy. In the end, I would be so very glad the customer came back and gave me that ten dollars!

This anecdote clearly illustrates that it makes perfect sense to treat others as you would like to be treated. The gas station attendant could have lost his job because of a simple error. As he was a middle-aged man, he was surely supporting a family and most likely was just barely getting by. Judging by his thankfulness when I came back in, who knows what repercussions he could have faced if I hadn't been so honest? The obvious benefit of being kind, honest, and loving to others is to affect positively those around us.

In another way, on a deeper level, helping and being kind and loving to others also has a positive effect upon us. As we proceed through life, we expect others to treat us in the same manner in which we treat them. If we treat others in a loving, kind, and honest way, we expect the same from them in return. This is how I view life. I try to treat others with honesty, kindness, and respect, and I expect the same back from them. Of course, I don't always get back in return that which I put forth, but I see this as an anomaly. When this happens, I think to myself, "This person is probably just having a bad day or going through a rough time, and I don't need to judge him or her. I just hope things are better for him or her in the future."

Because I live my life this way, I really do expect others to treat me as I treat them. For example, if I accidentally leave my wallet, keys, or some other personal item at a public place, such as an airport or mall, I expect it to be there when I get back or for someone to have turned it in. And this is usually the case—my misplaced item is almost always returned or waiting in the same spot for me. In truth, this doesn't happen 100 percent of the time. However, I try not to worry about those few times when I don't get my item back. When I am not reunited with my item, I think to myself, "That's how life rolls. Sometimes we lose things, but most of the time things turn out pretty well." Because I sincerely try to treat others well, this positive energy that I put out comes back to me more often than not.

I'm not deluding myself. Things might be stolen from me, and people might be dishonest to me. But neither happens that often to me, and I simply don't waste a lot of time and energy thinking about it. I honestly think that people are mostly like me, and so I expect people to treat me kindly in return. Because I see life this way, this is how I experience it. If I go to the store and the clerk is somewhat rude, I just say, "Hmm, he must be having a bad day. Maybe I can do something to make it better," and sometimes I can. Of course, sometimes I can't, but that's just how life is. The important thing is that I'm not going to let another person's bad day ruin my day. That would be silly! I'd much rather have a good day, keep positive, and be happy.

If we treat others in a kind, loving way, then we can expect others to treat us similarly and we can increase our chances of being happy. Of course, other people will not always reciprocate our positive energy, but our expectations will increase the odds of it happening. We'll begin to be attracted only to those people who treat us similarly. With time, we'll start surrounding ourselves with kind, loving, and honest people.

If someone were to cheat me or to be dishonest with me, I would say, "Well, that's too bad." Rather than dwelling upon the situation or letting the negativity ruin my day, I would take it as a learning opportunity, and in all likelihood, would cease to socialize with the person. As I go through life, I expect people to be honest, kind, and loving. I am more surprised when they don't act this way. I expect other people to be honest, kind, and loving and this usually makes my day and my life go pretty well.

There are many benefits of being kind, honest, and loving to others. You never know what the full effect of the kindness you show towards others may be. One of my favorite sayings is, "If you pull a blade of grass, the entire universe shakes." We can never predict what will happen when we reach out to others with kindness and love. Our actions might produce truly extraordinary results. If we're going through our day reaching out with kindness, love, and honesty, we may indeed be shaking the entire universe.

When we act with honesty, kindness, and love, then we will begin to expect the people around us to do the same. Because of this, we'll start surrounding ourselves with people who are honest, kind, and loving, even in new situations. Life will begin to flow much better. Life won't be so much, "My dukes are up. Don't get too close, to me or I'll punch you," but instead will be more like, "I love you. I sure would like to give you a hug."

Be loving, kind, and honest to other people, and see how most people reciprocate with positivity and how your life flows much better.

Chapter Forty-Eight
How to Plan for the Future without Missing Out on Today

One barrier that can keep us from happiness is delayed gratification. We tell ourselves, "Someday I'll . . . ." Even I do this.

When I started working and seeing clients over twenty-five years ago, a financial planner contacted me and told me that if I saved my money, invested it wisely, retired thirty to forty years later, I would have enough money that I wouldn't have to worry about working anymore. I wasn't necessarily planning on retiring, but I did like the idea of financial freedom. So I started to think about ways I could save money, putting it into an investment plan so someday I could have all the time, freedom, and money I needed to sustain myself and my kids so I wouldn't need to work anymore. I could work, but I wouldn't have to work. I spent a lot of time thinking about that. I'm pretty good at delayed gratification and putting things off for the future.

After finishing high school, I went through another fourteen years of schooling before I even started working full-time in private practice, so I was pretty good about waiting for the future. Unfortunately, I was too good at it, and in the process of now waiting for retirement, I wasn't living nearly fully as much as I should have been. I was very fortunate that I was able to learn this lesson well before retirement and didn't miss out on enjoying these past twenty years. But I did have to learn it—how to live now and plan for the future.

How do we live now and plan for the future? It's really one of the key factors of leading a happy life. If we're always planning for the future, then we're not living in the the moment. Living in the now, day by day, week by week, year by year, creates a beautiful life. When we look back on our life, we can say, "Yes, we're enjoying our retirement, and we enjoyed the journey getting here."

To find happiness, live in the now, and enjoy the journey of life, we need to make sure that every day is a special day, one that we can look back on at the end as we put our heads on our pillows and say,

"If I don't wake up tomorrow morning, it's okay because that was a good day!" The truth is we really don't know if we're going to wake up tomorrow morning, so it's important each day to make sure there are special things throughout our day, today, that make it a beautiful.

Yes, we still plan for the future, but we make sure that if today is our last day it's a good day. And no, we don't chuck everything that we invested in and go live a crazy day and then have to deal with a financial mess tomorrow. That's not what I'm talking about. Instead, we make sure that every day is one worth living, that we're not counting too much on living a life of "someday, I'll . . ." but do live each day fully.

It's very simple to do this, to live in the now and make each day worth living. At the beginning of each day and throughout the day, we say, "How do I make this a beautiful day?" We want to have moments throughout that are truly wonderful so it ends as a very rich and full day.

Let me share examples of what I do, and together, we'll explore some things you could do to make your day a beautiful one. Mind you these scenarios do change for me; what I'm doing now might change from what I'm doing six months from now, or even next week. These are the things I do pretty much every day that give me pleasure and put a smile on my face so that when I put my head down at the end of the day I say, "This was a good day."

For me, my family is very important to me. With my children, I get the benefit of taking them to school every day, which is something I really enjoy. For my daughter's class, I get to stay about fifteen minutes and read to the kids, which is a special time for my daughter and me to share together. I schedule my work a little later in the day to make room for my children in the morning and to have time to walk along Laguna Beach on my way to work. This beach is one of the most beautiful places in the world, and I really enjoy watching the waves and ocean every day.

Throughout my day, I do many other things to appreciate each moment. I enjoy meditating and do that in the morning when I first get up and again in the evening when I go to bed. When I eat, I spend time eating very slowly to appreciate them fully, so when I have my morning juice and my afternoon salad, I really enjoy them.

I have readjusted my schedule many times throughout my life and will continue to do so as needed. When I change it, I still make room to enjoy the moment—I just find new things to make each day special and beautiful. For example, someday I won't be taking my kids to school. They'll be in college or working on their own, and then I'll be doing other things, and that's fine.

What can you do to make every day is special? If you enjoy the outdoors, make a point to be outside every day if that works for you. Listening to beautiful music that's uplifting and positive can be very healthy. Connecting with friends and just stopping for a moment to talk can make our day special. Most things that I do don't cost me any money, and yet they often give me the greatest pleasure in being in the moment right now. So find those things that work for you and make them part of your life every day.

Now there is a caveat here. Some things we do might seem to enrich our lives and make our days special, but they're actually harmful. Addictions an obvious example. Everyone knows that drugs are unhealthy for us, but still people are addicted to drugs and do them because they want to have a good time. How we know something isn't good for us is by their after-effects. What do we feel like after we do it? Does it uplift us? Does it uplift the people around us? Or does it tear us down and maybe even hurt other people?

Other examples of addiction we might not recognize so easily. For example, we watch TV shows, movies, and listen to music that, at the end of a long day, can seem enjoyable, but they don't add anything positive to our lives. These forms of entertainment might be making fun of people, putting us in a sad mood, or showing dark images that get planted inside our head or put words in our mind that are harmful. Like drugs, they seem like something we enjoy doing, but we can tell they're not really good for us and they hurt us in the long run. We need to stay away from those types of things.

Another example is eating to excess or eating foods we know are not healthy. Eating food that tastes so good and is rich but is not good for us can later lead to gout or obesity. Eventually, such addictions can hurt us physically and even emotionally. Instead, finding foods that are good for us and eating them with pleasure is best.

You have to be the one determining what is or isn't good for you; nobody else can decide for you. Look at how it affects you in the short and long term.

Now the reverse can also be true. For example, if someone is a couch potato and starts moving around and perhaps walking outside regularly, it may initially cause some pain and soreness. However, a little bit of sensible reasoning will tell us that stretching our bodies, getting outside, spending time in nature, and moving around are really good for us. There might be a slight adjustment period, but once we start doing things that are good for us, put a smile on our face, and make us say, "This was a good day. I enjoyed today," they are going to be beneficial to us in the long run.

Every day in our life is not going to be blissful. But since we don't know what tomorrow is going to bring—or if it will come at all for us—we can only enjoy today. We make sure every day has beauty in it, so when we look back on the day we can say, "This was a good day." This is what our key to happiness is going to be. If we do this, if we make sure we can rest our heads each night and say those words, then we will find happiness in the now. If we can do this daily and stop putting things off until "someday I'll . . .," we end up with a string of beautiful days making a necklace of a wonderful life.

It's in our hands whether or not we have a happy life. All we have to do is right now, today, decide on making it a good day and letting tomorrow worry about tomorrow. If we do this instead of saying, "Someday I'll live life," we end up living life now and creating happiness for ourselves and those around us.

It's very simple; all we have to do is actually do it one day at a time—just today. Tomorrow, we'll do it again, but we won't worry about that now; we just do it today. Each day, we create one good day, and then we will find we've strung together a life that is happy.

Imagine we have a bow and arrow and are aiming at a target. The farther we stand away from the target and aim at it, the harder it is to hit. So if we get right up to the target and aim at the center of that circle, which represents happiness, then we're going to hit it. Being very close to the target represents "today," while being far away represents far in the future, and standing almost out of sight of the target is like saying, "Someday I'll . . ." The farther we move back, the harder it is to hit that happiness target; but if we stand right up to it, then we're probably going to hit it. We don't know what the future holds, and from a distance, we don't know if we can hit the target. But we do have confidence in hitting the bull's eye of happiness when we stand right in front of it. Each day, we can do that—walk up to the target and become the grand master of archery, the grand master of happiness.

Happiness is very easy to find as long as we look for it right here, right now. Let's focus on being happy today. That is a target we can all hit. Tomorrow when we get up and it's our new today, we'll do the same thing again. Happiness is something we can all have right now.

Chapter Forty-Nine
Death in Yellowstone:
Adjusting to the Impermanence of Life

Life is impermanent; nothing stays the same. We never know when tragedy might strike.

When I was vacationing in Yellowstone, the news reported a bear attack on a married couple. While hiking, the man and woman unwittingly got between a mother bear and her cub. They were both attacked; the husband was killed, and his wife barely survived with multiple injuries. This was the first time something of this nature had happened in over twenty-five years.

Additionally, while I was there, I visited many hot springs and noticed numerous signs posted warning people to be careful. The signs stated that if you ventured off the path, you risked falling into a hot spring. These signs had been paid for by a foundation set up by the family of a nine-year-old boy who had strayed off the path, fallen into one of the hot springs, and died.

Examples of the impermanence of life surround us. We can be happily married, enjoying a romantic hike, and our spouse can be killed by a grizzly bear. We can be on vacation with our family, and our child could fall into a hot spring and die. I know these are extreme cases, but tragedy of some sort strikes most of us at some time. Nothing stays the same in life. Life is bound to change. If we try to make life stay the same, we are going to suffer.

Sometimes these changes are good, but sometimes they are very painful. If we don't learn to roll with life, to adjust to the constant changes, then we are going to suffer. Impermanence is an absolute guarantee in life. No matter what is happening in our lives right now, it's going to change. Along life's journey, we will experience many changes. A large number of us are going to get divorced. Currently in America, the divorce rate is nearly 50 percent. Many of us will develop some type of cancer, heart disease, or other illness. We're going to get fired, our jobs are going to be downsized, our company will close, or something else will occur that will cause us to change jobs. In fact, many of us will be retrained and start all over on an entirely new career path. The average person in the United States will have six different jobs over the course of a lifetime. Life is change. Life is impermanent.

When facing change, we have only two choices regarding how to address them: we can deal with it, or we can mask it and ignore it. One choice is good for us, and the other choice is very bad for us.

To understand our choices and how they relate to change, think about getting a small wound or cut. When we get a small cut, we can wash and treat it and let it mend. Doing so may be a bit painful, but it will result in a healthy healing process. Or, we can simply take painkillers. The deeper and more intense the cut is, the stronger the painkillers will have to be. We can go on blissfully with our lives, not feeling our cut. However, if we do this without treating the wound properly, the cut will surely get infected, continue to get worse, and possibly even put our lives in danger. Ultimately, life with its constant changes is like this example. Unfortunately, most of us turn to painkillers instead of washing out that wound, dealing with that change, and moving on.

Consider marriage turned into divorce as another example of dealing with change. We're newly married, and we're excited by so many dreams, so many expectations of what life with our partner will bring. And then things don't exactly turn out the way we hoped. We find ourselves single again, perhaps having to raise children by ourselves, bogged down by financial stress and a myriad of worries. As we struggle with the effects of this change, we can deal our emotions and problems as they arise, or we can mask them.

To adjust to life's changes in a healthy way, we must allow ourselves to feel our feelings, get involved with support groups, talk to people, seek therapy, and deal with the sadness and anger of the divorce. Once we do so, we will feel better, and we will be able to heal and move on. We can do well when life presents a change, even when the change is tragic, as long as we are willing to adjust to the change, feel it, and then move forward.

However, in this situation, we may turn to the painkillers instead of dealing with our feelings. Unfortunately, we can use all sorts of painkillers to mask our feelings. Perhaps after the divorce we start drinking, and this drinking becomes a habit, which then turns into an addiction. We might ask a doctor for a prescription drug that takes away our anxiety, our stress, and our depression. We might throw ourselves into work or become addicted to television. We might dive into another relationship, putting all our time and effort and feeling into it, thinking this will fix us somehow. We might start eating excessively, turning to food for comfort. The list of what we can do instead of truly dealing with life's impermanence in the form of a divorce or any other change is infinite.

Most of us don't adjust well to life's impermanence. We fight it, we resist it, and we use painkillers as a way to deal with it. But if we realize at a deep level that life is impermanent and there's nothing we can do to get around this fact, we truly will be better off. We must flow with life, adjust to change well, and realize nothing we have in this world is a guarantee. Just as with the family who lost their child at Yellowstone, pain and tragedy can be turned into something wonderful and that can help others. The Yellowstone family is proof that we can adjust to anything and still find beauty and meaning in life.

Let me offer yet another example. Perhaps when we were in high school, we expected to attend college, get good grades, graduate, and get a great job, but this didn't happen. Instead, we didn't adjust to our newfound freedom, and we partied too much and mismanaged our time to such an extent that we had to drop out and get a job. This doesn't mean we have to numb ourselves to change. Life is change, and change happens to everyone. We need to feel, adjust, and then make the most of what life has given us. Wallowing in self-blame won't help. Yes, we may have been the cause of the change, but blaming ourselves won't help us to adjust and accept the change. We can adjust to anything, as long as we are willing to let go of our belief that life has to go a certain way. If we fight life, it will be very tough and we will most likely turn to addictions to shut off our pain. However, if we flow with life, then life will proceed much better, and we will be much healthier in the end.

Let's promise that no matter what life has thrown at us or will throw at us, we will adjust. We won't be self-critical, we won't stay stuck, and we won't numb ourselves to the pain. Instead, we'll feel the loss and sadness, and then we'll move on and make the most of our lives with what we have. When we adapt to change, we facilitate a beautiful, full, happy life.

Chapter Fifty
Facing Mortality and Being Happy

On a vacation in Peru, Lima's Monastery of San Francisco, begun in 1675, and the catacombs underneath it fascinated me. Approximately seventy thousand people are buried there, none with any identification. All these thousands of people are just thousands and thousands of bones and skulls, nameless in death.

The anonymity of those buried in the catacombs relates to our thoughts about death or, rather, what we refuse to face about death. Most of us pretend we'll live forever and be remembered just as long. Death won't come for us, we think. But the truth is it will for all of us. And in time, we too will be forgotten, just like those buried under the Monastery of San Francisco. We will be put to the ground, perhaps cremated, and eventually no one will be around who remembers us. Yet that absolute truth is something we have a hard time accepting. This is especially true when we're very young. The youth have a sense of invincibility; they feel nothing can harm them and they will live forever. Then, as we grow older and someone close to us dies, we realize we are vulnerable. But still, the thought of death remains distant, not something we want to think of about too deeply.

In my talking to people about the end of their life, I've learned most face death with the sense that it shouldn't happen to them. My visit to the catacombs in Lima reminded me that death is a fact for all of us. Even in as quickly as two or three generations, we will be forgotten. How many of us can go back more than four generations and say much about our ancestors? Unless they were famous, we are not going to remember them or know about their personalities. Even those who are well-known will someday enter oblivion.

The truth is that we are going to die, and facing that, really believing in that, is helpful in regards to happiness. It forces us to look at how we are living and put that in the perspective of our limited time on Earth. Are we living our lives well? Even if no one remembers us, even if we die tomorrow, how are we living now?

We tend to say, "If I live my life well and am remembered by other people, then I've done well because I made a difference." But out of all those seventy thousand humans whose bones were in the Monastery of San Francisco, not one of them has a story to tell. Today, there is nothing to remember any of them by. They may have been magnificent mothers, they may have been superb poets, they may have been world-class leaders, but not one is remembered anymore. So instead of thinking we should do things by which we will be remembered, we should choose another way to live our lives.

Let's say we're not going to be remembered by anybody. What do we have then? What we have is the ability and choice to live well now. If we live well now, if we accumulate a beautiful life that we enjoy, we will find happiness in the here and now, even if nothing is remembered about us. I think this is a beautiful way to live.

Of course, we want to prepare for the future. We may live for eternity; I still believe that, but we don't know. All we know is that we can live here and now well. That's something we can do. Focusing on the future—either believing we will live forever or in the next life—keeps us from living well today. I think that's why so many people struggle, because they forget that this is all we have. This life, this moment is the only guarantee we have because tomorrow the doctor may tell us we only have a few weeks to live. Tomorrow, a drunk driver can kill us. Tomorrow, our world could end. But TODAY at this moment, we are alive, and if we really believe that we are going to die, how much better can we live today? We can live so much better. When we really hold onto the truth that life isn't going to go on forever, we can believe it and savor every moment. I think this is the gift of death. Death can remind us to live well today. When we forget, we struggle. When we forget, we hang onto fears and anxieties, hopes and dreams that preclude us from living here and now well. The one thing that is guaranteed is that this life on planet Earth will end, and it isn't doing us any good not to think about it.

A better approach is to wake up each morning, saying this may be the last day we have to live, and then, throughout the day, appreciate every moment of each experience. We can say that the meal we're eating could be the last one we ever eat, our conversation with our children could be the last time we see them, the raindrops hitting the windows could be the last rain we ever hear. When we do that—and we can do that on a consistent basis—we fill our lives with joys and happiness that surpass any form of understanding because we will be living fully, knowing that our life may pass.

I have met many people diagnosed with incurable diseases, and they have told me they started to live once they knew they were going to die. We, too, can live well if we accept that we are going to die. We don't know when death may come. It could be today. Of course, we still prepare for the future, but we also should be living each day as if it's our last because it could be. We all know people who suddenly died without warning. If we start living as if each day is our last, we will find that it's very difficult to be anxious about the future or feel depressed if this is all we have and we love it. Instead of clutching to fame, fortune, or things we don't have, we celebrate what we do have. Maybe we're not with the love of our life, but we can celebrate what we do have, such as beauty all around us, good friends close by, or nature. Whether we're financially successful or not, it doesn't matter because we realize if we're not living well today, then we're not living.

We can have the whole world and be miserable. And we can have nothing yet be extremely happy if we live well right now. Living fully in this moment is one of the key factors of happiness. If we can remember this may be the last day we have to live, we will live better and happily throughout the day, whether or not it is our last. We can all live beautiful lives if we live as if today were our last.

Chapter Fifty-One
The Best Prayer:
How to Be Happy with God

This chapter on faith is applicable to everyone's journey towards happiness and does not require belief in God.

Many years ago when I attended university, I had the opportunity to spend a summer in the Middle East. After the summer ended, I was scheduled to fly home out of Cairo, Egypt. However, my plane was a full thirty-two hours late. I was exhausted and more than a little uneasy to learn that the delay had been caused by the necessity to fix mechanical problems the plane had suffered during its previous trip.

As we began to take off, the stewardess politely announced, "We should be arriving in Paris in a little over eight hours. *In sha' Allah.*" I had been in the Middle East long enough to be familiar with this phrase. The approximate translation is "God willing." Indeed, all faiths share this premise that, God willing, things will turn out a certain way. However, at that moment, her words weren't at all comforting to me. I desperately wanted to know that the plane had been repaired perfectly. I wanted to know with certainty that we would be arriving on time and safely because of the mechanics' excellent abilities, not "God willing."

All faiths share this premise that God is all-powerful, all-wise, and all-knowing. So we all have a sense of "give it to God and let go." For example, according to the Christian faith, Jesus taught his disciples The Lord's Prayer, which says, "Thy kingdom come, thy will be done, on earth as it is in heaven." Whether in the Christian tradition, "thy will be done," or in the Islamic, "in sha' Allah," the same premise is being expressed—the control is out of our hands.

When we pray, we have an opportunity to talk to God and share our concerns and our wants, which is what most people do. Whatever we say in our conversation with God, it usually relates to our happiness in some way. I'd like to teach you a prayer that is really the best prayer for happiness, whether you're experiencing hard times or enjoying good times. It goes back to "thy will be done" and relates to our attitude towards this principle.

If we believe God is all-powerful and in control, then we need to ask not that God's will be done but that we accept God's will in our hearts and are happy with it. If we do not believe in God, then once we do what we can, we accept the outcome and are happy with it. In either situation, believer or non-believer, we do our part well, but ultimately, we leave the outcome to whatever we believe is beyond us—God, the Universe, or luck. It's like that plane ride I had so many years ago. The stewardess hoped the mechanics had fixed the plane well and no misfortune would befall us, but ultimately our safe arrival in Paris was up to some greater force.

To be happy, we must accept that whatever does happen is God's will. We must accept not only that God's will is being done but also that whatever is being done is exactly what is supposed to be done. Of course, we do our part, and we do everything in our power to make our lives run smoothly. However, ultimately to be happy, we have to let go and say, "Hmmm, this is what's going on. I've done my best to rectify it, and all I can do now is leave the rest to God." Whatever that "rest" is, we have to accept it and be happy with it.

Let's say you want to gain acceptance into a prestigious university. You study extremely hard, and you score well on your exams, but the top three schools you wish to attend, Harvard, Princeton, and Yale, all turn you down. Although some other good universities are still available to you, you had your heart set on attending one of those three. If you wish to be happy, then you say, "God, I did my part and studied hard. I prayed I would be accepted into one of those three schools, but I wasn't. So I have to be happy with the one you send me to. Thank you, God, because I know thy will is being done." Life is like this; sometimes accepting the outcome of what is can be very difficult.

As another example, let's say that the doctor diagnoses your spouse with cancer. Of course, you're going to do everything in your power to help your spouse get well as soon as possible. But ultimately, to be happy, you have to accept the outcome of life after you've done your part. You have to say, "God's will is being done, even when I don't like it. If I want to be happy, then I have to accept that God's will is being done. Yes, I'm going to feel my feelings, and yes, I'm going to do my part. But, whatever the outcome is, even if I don't like it, I'm going to learn to accept it. I'm going to learn to accept what is and perhaps with time I'll even learn to love what is." I know this can be a scary concept, but this is about being happy. If we hang onto anything too tightly, we're going to suffer. We don't have to suffer! We can have a beautiful life, but we have to learn how to let go. We do our part, and we leave the rest to God. Whatever the outcome is, we learn to accept it and be happy.

I know this can be frightening, but if you are a person of faith, then you believe that God is in control. God could choose to make things better but has not, so we must accept what is.

I want to end with perhaps one of the best prayers I could ever teach you. If you pray it from the bottom of your heart, life will proceed a lot better, especially during the tough times. This prayer is: "God, whatever happens, help me accept whatever you give and be happy with it. Help me, God, to believe that whatever happens is your will. Your will is being done. Help me to accept what happens and love what happens. I may have things that I want, I may have preferences, but what I truly wish is to be happy after I do my part in whatever happens. I trust and know that what happens is exactly what you had in mind. Thank you, God, thank you."

I know this lesson can be a difficult one to learn. However, when we experience tough times, after we do what we can, it can be extremely helpful to hand the outcome over to God. We all can have beautiful lives when we let go and just live.

Chapter Fifty-Two
Henry David Thoreau:
"Simplify, Simplify"

Busy, busy, busy. Boy, can we be busy! We can be so active from the second our alarm goes off in the morning to the second we put our head down at night. By that time, we're exhausted.

We do so many different things and yet often we still don't feel as if we accomplished everything we set out to do that day. What's this all about? Where does busyness come from?

Although I don't think we can give credit to him for figuring it all out, Henry David Thoreau did make some great discoveries when he spent two years in the nineteenth century living by a lake called Walden Pond. The book he wrote, entitled *Walden*, describes the beauty of nature and how much of a wonderful time he had. In that book, Thoreau says, "Simplify, simplify." I think we often go through life exhausted because we take on too many things, bring too much complexity to our days, and don't have time to enjoy life. We are in need of simplifying our lives.

I learned this when I was in college, and it changed my life. One summer, I worked hard and saved two thousand dollars from my job, enough to go to Europe the next summer, where I rode a bike for three months and immersed myself in European culture. I had grown up in the Midwest where people worked hard and sometimes never took vacations. But in Europe, people often didn't work long periods. Instead, they would take time off for a long lunch and dinner, and they didn't work crazy schedules. I discovered that, although they might not have as much wealth or as many material possessions as people in America, they had more time to spend with family, enjoy their connections, be in nature, and travel. Suddenly, I saw I had an option other than what everyone was supposed to do. The norm in America said I should join the workforce, apply myself very hard for many years, and then, someday, have retirement when I could finally have time to enjoy myself. My newly realized option said I could get a job where I worked hard and, at the same time, enjoyed the journey of life. I would have to live on less if I did it that way, but I could enjoy life a lot more.

Seeing this option in the way Europeans lived changed my life, and I am thankful for the experience because I have practiced keeping my life simple since then. I have time to exercise, be with my friends, be in nature, travel, and so on. Of course, there are sacrifices because I work for myself. If I don't work, I don't get paid, so I am not making money while on vacation. However, I am enjoying myself in those times, and I would rather enjoy life than work all the time.

What I am doing is the opposite of what most Americans do. They that someday they'll be happy, be able to direct their life, and enjoy life. Their "someday" is after they reach a certain point in their life plans, usually retirement.

However, it is better to enjoy life now because we don't know what the future holds. Life is impermanent and full of unpredictability. If you enjoy life along the way, you are definitely going to be happier than if you are waiting for a specific time to begin enjoying it. Let's see how we can learn to do this from Henry David Thoreau's "Simplify, simplify" motto.

If our lives are full of activities—work or volunteering or other activities important to us—then time goes by very quickly, and we are going to miss out on a lot. We can start today to move our lives into something simpler while still doing what we must. Here are four steps to take to get us there:

1. Become aware of how we spend our time.
2. Identify what we can spend less time doing.
3. Say no to some requests.
4. Reduce some expenses.

First, we need to become self-aware. What are we doing? How busy are we throughout the day? We need to look at our lives and see all the activities we are doing—at work, for our families, for friends, with organizations, as well as on the computer and in front of the TV. How we are complicating our lives can be a subtle. We can fill our lives with anything. It's so easy to get home, log onto the computer to look something up, and then three hours have gone by. So we need to look closely at how we are spending all our time.

Second, we see what we could do less of. What often holds us back from eliminating some of our busyness is that we start making a certain amount of money, increase our spending to that level, and then feel we have to continue working at a certain pace to pay our bills and maintain our lifestyles. We might also be trying to keep up with the Joneses—and that level is higher than ever. Years ago in high school, for the prom, prizes were awarded, and one was a limousine that would take one couple to the event. My best friends won, and they were thrilled with it. Here in California where I live now, everyone who goes to the prom gets a limousine. It's expensive, but often people do it because everyone else is doing it and they want to keep up with everyone.

A lot of this pressure comes from the media. They tell us, "You need this really nice car," "You need to go to the prom in a limousine," "You need to have this big house, even if there are just two of you." Unfortunately, their messages teach us to keep financially trapped because we're trying to keep up with the Joneses. Some of the people I have worked with have tried to keep up with Joneses who owned multiple homes by buying more homes. We may think that's silly, but wherever we live, we all tend to keep up with other people who are nearby. And when we do that, we may keep up with them, but we're not having time to enjoy life. Instead, we're sacrificing our lives just to keep up with other people, so in a sense we're letting other people control our happiness. We sure don't want other people controlling our happiness. We would rather be the ones making the choices to decide how happy we're going to be.

Luckily, we can do this in a simple way. We need to realize that we can only do so many things in one day. We all know this, so we need to decide what is important. Is it going for a walk by the park? Is it spending time with family and friends? Is it taking care of our body physically by working out or taking a yoga class? If the answer is yes, then we need to make time for it, which means we need to be less busy in other areas.

The message we need to tell ourselves, replacing the ones from the media, is slow down and enjoy life more. What can we do less of that will let us enjoy life more? Maybe, we are an active member in church or kids' programs, but these busy things don't give us time for us to enjoy life. I'm not trying to encourage us to be selfish—it is wonderful to give to others. But we matter too! We need to have time to give to ourselves so that sometimes we can take a break for the day and spend time with nature. We can go on a short vacation, which is good for the soul. But if we're doing things for others all the time, then we're missing out on those opportunities to take time for ourselves. It's really about striking a balance—giving time to family, to work, to others, and to ourselves. When we do that life goes a lot better, but we have to simplify and let things go.

Third, we need to say no to some requests. This takes practice because, typically, when someone asks us a favor, we say yes. When we say yes to everything, there's no time to do things that are good for us, that contribute to our happiness, and we suffer. It's not that we have to say no to everything, but we have to decide what's important, say yes to those, and say no to the others. I had a professor when I was in graduate school that gave wise advice. He said it's good to help organizations but pick two and get actively involved in only these. When we limit ourselves, then we have time, and we can actually give more of ourselves without feeling as if small pieces of our effort are going to too many things haphazardly.

When our lives are too full, the balance is lost, and our self-care starts to suffer. It's hard to be happy if we are not making time for our self-care on a daily basis. Many moms end up with depression when they are raising their kids because they're so busy all the time doing things for everyone else that they have no time for themselves. They can still be great moms by making sure they are happy, by finding a balance between taking care of others and taking care of themselves. Likewise, I see a people finishing college who get their first jobs and put loads of effort into doing well. This often means putting in long hours at work. Unfortunately, this also means not having time to work out and to take care of themselves. Yet they get promoted and move up in their careers. There is a price tag on choices, and sometimes it's a high one.

This leads to the fourth step, reducing our expenses. If we don't want to pay the price for focusing on our career, we may have to accept a lower income. And that means adjusting our spending. Can we? If we have a lot of expenses, then we're going to have to go to work. We may not be able to take all our sick leave because we have to work and we need that little extra income because money is so tight. We may not be able to switch jobs if that's the right choice for us because we are living paycheck to paycheck. But if we begin to move in the opposite direction where we're not spending too much, then we start to have options. We can work in the direction of simplification.

This can be difficult if we hold onto those messages from the media always to reach for the newest, fanciest, best. For instance, I knew a couple where the husband wanted to get a new car to replace his old one. They were struggling financially, and I encouraged them to keep their car, but he was insistent on getting a new one. They sold the car to their neighbors, and ten years later, that car was still running well. If he had kept his car, he would have had fewer payments and thus more time for himself.

We may not get as far in our careers or on the pay scale or in other aspects of life when we simplify our lives. But we have better, more satisfying lives filled with quality instead of quantity. Not everyone will agree with this. Others may say it's more important doing many things and impressing people. But if you're reading this, it's probably because you have a different value. You want to be happy now, not someday. And, being happy now means making time for it. If our lives are simpler, if they aren't so full of different activities that we're giving to other people or work or whatever it may be, then we'll have time to smell the roses, and it's good when we do that. When we take time to enjoy simple pleasures, then we can have a happy, beautiful life.

There's another saying I like: We can have anything we want in life, but we can't have everything. So, if we want to do awesomely in our career and maybe become CEO of a company, it probably will be at the expense of other things. Most CEOs of Fortune 500 companies work hard, but their success comes with a price. When people come to the end of their life, they never say, "I wish I had spent more time at the office." Too many do say, "I wish I had spent more time with my family and friends." But if we take time now for ourselves to enjoy the journey of life, then when we're on our deathbed, we can say, "Wow, I had a great life."

To simplify our lives, first, we notice where our time is going. Next, we adjust it so it works best for us. Then, we say no to requests for our time; we don't have to take on so many activities. And last, we reduce our spending so we don't feel we have to give time to work that can prevent our enjoying life now.

We're probably not going to do what Henry David Thoreau did and live at a lake to make our lives simple. But we could move in that direction. We could get a smaller home. We could keep our cars a little bit longer. We might not go for that job promotion this year. We could take a vacation. We could say no to some of the volunteer requests we get. Maybe we won't sign our kids up for so many classes and simplify their life as well as ours. We can be very busy, but we also need time just to relax—to do nothing, take naps, meditate, walk around the block, and so on. Spending time in nature is great for our souls. That's one of the important messages in *Walden* —how beneficial the power of nature can be.

We do well when we simplify our lives and have time to be happy. Happiness is within our reach. So let's work towards making our lives simpler and making time to fill our cups with what gives us happiness.

Once you move in the direction of simplifying your life, you'll find you spend time on the core things that put a smile on your face, and your life will start to become amazing with less, not more. And you'll find less is actually more because your priorities are the things that are best for you.

Chapter Fifty-Three
Are You Numb to Pleasure?
How to See Life with New Eyes

Success can seem so wonderful. We're high on a cloud for having achieved what we aimed for and feel everything else in our lives should be great. Unfortunately, success can have a downside. When we succeed financially, we might start possessing more things, and they can start to possess us. We expect or need them to provide a sense of contentment. To keep from letting them rule our lives, we need to put several ideas into practice.

- We have a variety of experiences to keep one thing from ruling our lives.
- The variety includes simple pleasures.
- We appreciate everything we have and enjoy all we do.

Let me use food to illustrate this. When I moved to California, I got into the habit of eating gourmet pizzas. I didn't pay attention to how they tasted; I only cared about going to what everyone considered the best pizza place in town every time I ate. After a while, even the best began to lose its appeal because now there's the best of the best and the best of the best of the best. When we get try to get the best, without thinking about whether we are enjoying them, we are chasing after what someone else has decided we should have. And that doesn't satisfy us in the end. We lose the pleasure of life.

We need to learn to say yes to enjoying what truly gives us pleasure and seeking that experience in the simpler activities. We should maintain that childlike approach to living because when we move up the ladder of success and start eating fancy foods or living in nicer places or driving more luxurious cars, those activities or possessions might not give us the pleasure we expected. This is a subtle change that happens. Those things we choose become requirements. We feel we have to have those things—they're part of our achieving that success—and so we lose out on their enjoyment.

People start getting so used to having rich things that they feel they need them, without enjoying them anymore.

When someone is very hungry, as I was in college when I had little money, going out to a fast-food place once a month becomes a great pleasure. You enjoy yourself. The food is great, and I remember when I ate it I really enjoyed it. Food never tasted so good. Now, I still try to cultivate pleasure when eating. I allow myself to eat rich food only on weekends and eat raw foods during the week. I really enjoy my food. It's a great balance, and that's what we want to work towards so that if life along the way does take away those rich things from us, we will be okay.

Let me use another example. Sometimes, I work with clients that do very well financially and have many expensive possessions, even several beautiful homes. But sadly, they get used to all they have. After a time, those things do not make them happy anymore; those possessions are just requirements for their level of income. Still, these people might think, "I need a home overlooking the ocean, and then I'll be happy again."

If we're not careful, this can happen to us on a lesser level. We can get used to things we have that should be considered blessings. We forget to be grateful for what we have and, instead, start looking for what more we should get. And then, if these things we do have go away, they can cause us a great deal of stress, anxiety, and suffering. So the key is we have to see everything in life, even our health, as a gift.

Think about when we're hanging onto something so tightly. We have to have that first-class seat in the plane; we have to have that four-thousand-square-feet home; or we have to have a luxury vehicle. Then when we do get it, we're holding onto it so tightly that we're not even enjoying it. We think we need things just so we can feel okay, and then we miss out on the gift they are in our lives.

If we enjoy traveling, we might have started off staying at inexpensive motels. Then we moved up to hotels and maybe even progressed to luxury resorts. That's great, but it's sad if the luxury resort becomes something we have to have just to feel content. Instead, we should see staying there as a blessing. Then, we're not only successful but also really enjoying it in the present moment. It's about seeing what we do have for the blessings they are. Life is a blessing.

When we define happiness, we have to keep it very childlike. If we see things with raw, beginner eyes, we will be able to enjoy life. When we say that we have to have certain things in order to be content, we are setting ourselves up for suffering because they will not always last. If, instead, we can say we're going to enjoy staying in palaces but also enjoy staying in a tent when we go camping, then we can enjoy every single experience because we're ready for and willing to enjoy anything. Then this spectrum of life becomes something that is beautiful, no matter what life gives us.

So why do we get so easily attached to things and feel we need them in order to feel content? This happens for two reasons:

1. We enjoy the physical sensation they give us.
2. We care what others think about us, our possessions, and our actions.

First, our physiological sensations tell us what feels or tastes or sounds good. It feels nice to lie on a fluffy bed. Salt and butter and rich cream taste so much better than raw carrots and greens with no seasoning on them. An expensive car runs smoothly and almost soundlessly. Of course, there's truth to those statements, but the freedom from attachment to them comes from saying we don't need them. We'll go camping, or we'll stay at a luxury resort. Either is okay. We'll see both options as a gift. But when we get used to these things and, for instance, say rich food is better and we want only it, this can bring with it some negative consequences.

We can take drug addicts as an example. People do drugs like heroin and crack because it makes them feel wonderful, but we don't do them because we know their great positive feelings come with great negative consequences. Addictions are very destructive, overwhelming the person to have the drug's pleasurable sensation over and over at any cost. In studies when rats have parts of their brains stimulated in a positive way, they want that stimulation nonstop. They can die from starvation, as long as they have the sensation.

Although we may not have drug addictions, we sometimes act as if we are addicted by focusing on a single activity—and then needing a higher and higher level of that—to bring us pleasure all the time. For example, always indulging in food pleasures can cause us to become obese or get illnesses, such as diabetes or gout. When we need certain things to feel pleasure all the time, we lose out on truly enjoying life; we are focusing on acquiring more and more of that one pleasure and are not appreciating it and not enjoying anything else in our life. We have to find a balance in enjoying all that life gives us and not demand only more and more of one pleasure.

When we're balanced, we do a lot better. I have a sweet tooth and especially love chocolate, but I eat it in moderation and balance that indulgence with a healthful diet otherwise. Fruits and vegetables fill many of my meals, and I enjoy them as much as the chocolate. Eating a variety of foods lets me remember how good food tastes when I switch to a different one. Even chocolate all the time loses its pleasure. It's about balance.

There's really nothing wrong with having material things, staying in nice places, or living in nice homes. But the key is we must see each as a gift, be thankful when we have it, and be okay when we don't. Having the variety allows us to appreciate the different experience—different from the one we just had—even if we've done it or had it before. The contrast between them lets us see the more recent experience almost as if it's new. Even heroin addicts get this trick: they will often quit heroin for a week or two before returning to the habit, just so they can feel the high, the rush of the seemingly first time of doing heroin again. Though we're not heroin addicts, the idea is that it's important not to have only one thing all the time.

We need to work towards balance and seeing everything as a blessing, saying to ourselves, "I'm glad to have this now. Is it good for me in the long run?" If it isn't, then we focus on having it only some of the time to avoid becoming addicted to this one pleasure. If we become used to things, we start missing out on the pleasure that we have been given from them.

Second, letting others influence our decisions is an equally powerful reason for our attachment to things. We care about what other people think, so we get that nicer car. Unfortunately, by focusing on others' opinions, we're giving them power over our happiness. And that has nothing to do with our enjoyment of what we are getting; it has to do with asking ourselves, "What will other people think?" When we care too much about what other people will think, we are going to suffer. Freedom comes from living life because we just want to. If today we want to live in a palace and tomorrow we want to rent a small apartment and go work for the Peace Corps, that's great. But we have to do it because we really want to, not because of what others think about it.

A fellow I knew illustrates this idea. He bought a very expensive car, but after about three months, he told me that he got used it. It was just another car. He kept it only because of the accolades he would get from other people who were so impressed with it. But the car caused him a lot of financial stress. So it didn't bring him any pleasure; it only brought him the pleasure of giving other people the chance to be impressed by it.

That's sad, but many of us have the same attitude about things. We get them not so much because we enjoy them but, instead, to impress others. We become puppets to other people's opinions of us. Those puppet strings need to be cut. If we want to have nice things, eat at gourmet restaurants, stay in luxury hotels, or so on, there is nothing wrong with that, but we shouldn't be doing it to impress others. Otherwise, we are depending on their praise and approval, and people's opinions change all the time. We can go up and down in the opinion polls of others very quickly, so it's best not to pay much attention to them. To impress others is never-ending.

It's best if we do things just because we enjoy doing them, rather than because we're trying to impress the world. If people like what we're doing, that's great, but we're not swayed by their opinion. If circumstances change, as life does change, we can also change. We won't be swayed by people's negative opinions of us when we don't live in that nice house anymore or if we don't have our fancy car. So, as much as we don't let others control us when we're doing well, we also don't let them control us when we're not doing well in their eyes. We just do things for the sake of doing them and because we want to. Then we're free! We're free to flow with life. When it's a good day, great. When we're not doing as well, it's still great. It doesn't matter, because there's always something beautiful that we can be with.

We can have the most amazing life, if we live in the present moment without being attached or focused on the future; not being stuck in the past, just living in the now and seeing everything with those beginner eyes. The beginner eyes see everything as gifts, as something new that we're going to be with every time.

If we see everything as new, we really enjoy our time with people we care about, we enjoy the food we eat, and everything else becomes so much more enjoyable. We won't care about what other people think, and we will allow ourselves to adjust to life's changes and go with the flow. We can flow with the beauty of life. We can love the gifts we've been given, no matter what comes our way because there is always something beautiful.

Chapter Fifty-Four
Life Can Be a Permanent Vacation

Boy, oh boy, can we struggle! We can get upset when things don't go the way we want them to. We can be upset when things change. And we hate it when something that was going well changes and starts going south. Someone we love has left. Our job has suddenly ended. Or an illness has kicked in. There are so many different ways we can suffer.

But we don't need to suffer so. We can learn something from vacations, apply it, and make the rest of our lives a lot better.

Vacations are so relaxing, they give us a chance to see different parts of our world, and they allow us to meet new people. But what do vacations have to do with happiness and not suffering?

One of the key factors is that we don't own much that has to do with the vacation. We don't own the plane that flies us to our city of choice; we don't own the car that takes us from the airport to our destination; we don't own the hotel room. Everything we use will have to be given back; we know that and are perfectly happy with this arrangement. Because we're not attached to these, we don't get upset when we leave.

But now, if someone says, "I'm going to take your home next year," we can be devastated. When we're on vacation and get reminded we need to check out so someone else can use the room, we don't get upset. We're very fine with that, and we just move out and go somewhere else. That's the key. Since we're not attached to anything during our vacation, we just flow with life and have a great time. The minute we get home, however, we start getting attached to things again. We expect them to be there, and if they're not, we become upset.

For a moment imagine if we saw life as a vacation where nothing we have was ours. Someone else will want our house or want our job or want a lot of things that we have. I know it may seem silly, but when we view life like this, we stop being so attached to everything. If and when change comes (and some change is inevitable), we won't be so destroyed or upset by it because we're not clinging to it.

It's like when we are asked to check out of the hotel room: we're not upset because we're not clinging to the room.

When I was younger, I didn't own anything except for clothes, my bag, and a few other things. Yet I wasn't worried. I just realized there would be a time when I would be able to purchase things, and I would get by. But, when we get older, we think we need certain things to be okay, so we become attached to them. Then we get upset if we think they're going to be taken away from us.

Attachment and clinging cause us to suffer. We spend a lot of time fearful of things being taken away because we're attached to them. No matter what, we want them to be there for the rest of our lives, but that makes life dangerous because we're clinging tightly to something that probably is going to change. Even if the change doesn't happen, we will still cause ourselves to suffer by worrying about that possibility.

If we start seeing life as a vacation where nothing belongs to us, we stop holding onto things. Then when things change, we can handle that because we're not attached to them being the same way all the time. And we're actually going to enjoy what we have in a greater way. On vacation, we're able to have a really nice time with all the comforts we don't have at home, and we allow ourselves to enjoy it because we know it's not there forever. If we do the same with what we have at home, guess what? We will begin to enjoy everything so much more because we don't own it. Rather, we see it as a gift.

For example, we can wake up every morning and say, "What a great place I have to live in today. I don't know about tomorrow, but I sure am blessed today." When we do that, life is a better experience because we're not attached, and we enjoy what we have. We enjoy vacations, even though they're not permanent, and we're okay with that. We're fine with it because we're not attached.

Sometimes we stay in nice hotels; sometimes we stay in less nice hotels. Whatever happens, we adjust to those changes because we're on vacation. If we have the same attitude in the rest of our lives, we will find happiness. We can say, "I'm on vacation for the rest of my life," and then we'll have better lives. When we are on vacation and things don't go the way we want them to, we handle it better because we don't expect things to stay the same. By losing the expectation and attachment, when changes happen, we can just roll with them and have a good time. Sometimes things go well, and sometimes they don't go the way we want. But we can adjust to them. As long as we don't cling to them, we are okay.

Losing attachment also applies to people. The reality is they sometimes leave too. People we love might die, someone we're dating could leave the relationship, or a friend could move to a distant city. If we cling to other people, then we're going to suffer. Instead, if we see them as part of our vacation, then we can enjoy them the way we would when meeting new people during a holiday without expecting to see them again. We're going to have a great time with them, but we don't expect to have them in our lives forever. Because of this impermanence, we can really enjoy their company. This may be harder to do with people we love, but the results are going to be the same. If we don't cling to people when they come home late one night, we're not going to freak out. When tragedy does strike and our relationship ends through death or a breakup, we will be okay. Of course, there will be some suffering, but a lot less. The less we cling, the less we suffer.

We have a choice. Do we want to be happy, or do we want to suffer? Sometimes relationships end, but even if they're not ending, the fear of change is there. We might have a fight with our partner and think the relationship is over and we're going to be miserable for the rest of our lives. Or, if our child has a cough, we might think she's going to die from a serious illness. Our minds have the tendency to create stories of the worst that can happen when we cling to things and people. Even if they do happen, we deal terribly with the situation because we have clung so tightly that we can't let go.

Now, imagine if we did this with our pets. Every time I get a new pet, I realize it's probably going to pass away before I do. The dogs or cats or other pets most of us have don't live as long as people. But that doesn't keep us from loving them. We may love them even more, in fact. Think about going to the house of someone who has pets and enjoying them. When we leave, we don't have suffer.

When we see other people as being on vacation with us and we don't know how long we get to travel with them, life will go better.

Sometimes our paths with other people stay on the same journey for a long time, but other times they quickly go separate ways. That's okay because we're not clinging; we're not expecting anything. We might be hopeful they will stay with us, but we're not attached. Not clinging to them will cause us to find happiness because we will enjoy our time and then deal better should changes occur. We don't love deeply out of a fear of losing the person. So, not clinging to someone causes us to love them better when they are in our lives. This is a possibility for any of us.

Unfortunately, people want to hang onto things and call them mine, mine, mine. When we cling to things, we can't enjoy them because it's as if we're in the military defending our country. If we're protecting an empire, we are not going to be enjoying the place; instead, we will be focused on it how to keep from losing it to others. To enjoy things, we have to let go and just see them as a gift for the day. If changes come, we can enjoy those, too.

This idea of letting go applies to our health as well. How do we not cling to our good health and, instead, see that as part of the vacation? It goes back to expectations. We like to be physically healthy and fit all the time. But we're not. When we get sick, we might create stories about it, such as, "This isn't supposed to be happening; I'm supposed to be healthy all the time." But look at athletes and how they handle pain. They are sore a lot of the time. Yet they continue playing and competing and actually choose to do the activities that cause their bodies pain. But they are not attached to being free of pain; they accept the pain, even choose to live this way. It's as if they're on vacation. They're not thinking that life has to be perfect all the time.

When we feel we have to be perfect all the time, we bring suffering into our lives. I knew someone who used to struggle with alcoholism, and when she quit, she told me her body was hurting a lot. When she was drinking, she didn't feel much bodily pain. I think that's probably why people turn to addictions: they want to mask the pain and feel good all the time. If we don't get attached to being always free of pain and, rather, see physical pain as just part of life, we cope better. If we can roll with the changes, then we can still enjoy life.

Here's another little subset within not being attached. We can focus on only one thing at a time. So let's say we're on vacation, and the weather is horrible. We can't get outside at all. We were planning on lying by the pool and reading all day, but instead, we have to read in our rooms. This is okay because there are also other things we can do, such as get a massage at the spa. So we have a choice: we can focus on the bad weather and how we can't follow our plans, or we can focus on the other activities we can do instead. We can't focus on both, so we have to decide on only one. So which do we choose—the negative or the positive?

It's the same way with health. If we are sick, we can watch TV or read a book, or we can call our friends and (if we're not contagious) have them come over. The point is that we can adjust to anything if we are not attached to a certain outcome. We don't want to be sick or suffering physically, of course, but when we are ill or in pain, our minds can make things either worse or better. If we focus on the good things in our life, we're not going to focus on the bad things as much. Look at people who are battling severe depression. When they watch a comedy movie, they are not depressed. They might only feel depressed when they return to their heads after the movie. We can always choose to feel good and concentrate on something beautiful.

We just have to see it as not permanent and not become attached to it. When I was younger, I used to go on backpacking trips for over a week. They involved walking all day long, and by the end of the day, I was sore. Sometimes I had blisters and aches all over. However, I chose to go on those long hikes with significant pain because I was focused on the beauty and tranquility of being in nature. Since I love nature so much, I was willing to put up with the pain.

When we are suffering, we still have choices. We can choose to suffer. Or we can choose to feel we are on vacation and focus on the things around us that are beautiful. We won't plan on them being there forever, and then we'll discover that happiness is just a natural state on which we don't lay a claim. We can all have beautiful and happy lives when we see life as a vacation.

Chapter Fifty-Five
The Consequence of
Not Pursuing Happiness

In spite of all the tragedies and sadness in the world, happiness *is* possible. Regardless of our circumstances, we can find and keep happiness in our lives. But we must make pursuing happiness central to our lives.

About twenty years ago when I first started in private practice, I had a young man come to me who was so amazingly intelligent, bright, and alive with life. Although he was an incredible pleasure to work with, he came from a background where there was a lot of pain, a lot of suffering, and a lot of darkness.

As we worked together for roughly six months, he was on an uphill trajectory. However, circumstances changed, and he stopped coming to therapy. He got involved in other things, and he ceased working on himself and his pursuit of happiness.

About seven years later, I was leaving my office one evening, and he was there waiting for me. He just wanted to talk to me for a few minutes. Clearly, life hadn't gone well for him, and although I could see hints of his former self, most of him wasn't there anymore. Life had been hard on him, and he had transformed into a completely different person. After he left, I cried in my car. I truly felt sorry for the way his life had turned out because he was such a beautiful soul. Especially because he had come from such a challenging background, it didn't take long for him to deteriorate to such an extent that he was barely recognizable.

Although we may not have a background as challenging as this young man's, this anecdote does relate to us all. If we don't pursue happiness, then we end up in other places that cause us misery and suffering. We must continue to put energy toward the pursuit of happiness.

We all understand this idea when we apply it to our health. If we always put forth energy to eat well, exercise, refrain from smoking, and limit alcohol, then we'll age pretty well, as long as we don't endure any major physical catastrophe. The same applies to happiness: if we make the effort to be happy, we will be happy—and more. Unlike health, happiness doesn't have to decline as we get older. We can gradually grow in our state of happiness and become happier as we age.

We have two choices. We can take time to be happy and then have a happy life, or we can put our time elsewhere and then get out of "happiness shape." Happiness takes effort, and if we don't work at it, I can guarantee we are going to become unhappier as we age. We may mask this unhappiness with addictions, such as alcohol or prescriptions drugs, but we are going to become unhappier unless we work at it.

Why will we become unhappier unless we continue to pursue happiness? One reason may be our background. Unless we had the most loving, perfect parents in the world and grew up in a beautiful, perfect environment, chances are we have some healing to do. If we don't take the time to heal and fix the conditioning of our past, then we will have a tendency toward unhappiness.

A second reason is perhaps more subtle, but it definitely exists. Our world really isn't invested in us being happy; our world is far more invested in itself and its own gain, and that often involves pain and suffering.

I experienced this when I was part of a ten-part series with the Fox Reality Channel. My role in the series was to help the participants understand why they were acting as they were. As always, I explained each individual's behavior in a kind and loving way because I believe there are always underlying reasons as to why we do things. The director was constantly trying to have me say things that I wasn't comfortable with, and after six weeks, they fired me because I wasn't sensational enough. Yes, I got fired from a show called *Busted and Disgusted* because I wouldn't attack people and make fun of them! Unfortunately, happy stories with happy images throughout the entire program didn't sell well. Most people who watch TV or movies want drama, excitement, and to see people get hurt, and this is what the media are pushing today.

These images shape us and affect the way we interact with the world. If we watch these types of images enough and take in the negative themes in news events, TV, radio, movies, music, and so on, they will wear us down. They make us become cynical and lose faith in humanity; we become far from happy.

Check this out for yourself. If anyone you know watches a lot of news, is he or she happy? I doubt it. And if you're watching the news every single day, waking up daily to all the negative news events, you need to STOP! Instead, go for a walk, spend some time in nature, watch the sunrise, or listen to the birds and see if your day or even your week doesn't go a little bit better. Take this challenge in order to determine if you don't feel happier in life with fewer negative messages and more positive and beautiful surroundings.

This is the other path we can choose, a path where we're surrounding ourselves with things that add to our happiness. Such things clearly make us more positive, more peaceful, and happier people. Meditation is one of the big ones that we can choose. You would be hard-pressed to meditate and not find that, with time, you become happier. A number of scientific studies support this fact.

My goal here isn't to explore every aspect of happiness and unhappiness, but instead to look at the overall picture. If we actively pursue happiness, then we are going to become happier. When we work at something, we're going to achieve positive results.

However, the reverse is also true, and it's far more subtle. If we do not work toward achieving happiness, then we will inevitably become unhappy. For example, if we want financial security and we're poor, then we have to work at it. The poorer we are, the more work it takes to become make money. But sooner or later, we will become wealthier, especially if we have someone knowledgeable helping us along the way. But if we don't work at it, we're going to lose out and not reach our goal. If we just sit around and do nothing, money is not going to come to us. The same is true for happiness. If we don't do anything to become happy, then we are going to end up being unhappy because of the many things in life pushing against us negatively. If we want to be happy, we have to work at it.

Happiness is something we can all have, no matter what our backgrounds are or how old we may be. We can all work toward happiness. It takes work, but achieving happiness is so worth the effort.

About Dr. Robert Puff

Dr. Robert Puff, PhD is a clinical psychologist, author, international speaker, and happiness expert who has been counseling individuals, families, non-profits, and businesses for over twenty-five years (www.DoctorPuff.com). A contributing writer to *Psychology Today*, he has authored numerous books and creates a weekly podcast on happiness at www.HappinessPodcast.org. If you are interested in having Dr. Puff speak at your organization or company, you can learn more about his speaking services at www.SuccessBeyondYourImagination.com.

CPSIA information can be obtained
at www.ICGtesting.com
Printed in the USA
FSOW01n0351201115
13597FS

9 781456 625801